Do's and Taboos
Around The World

3rd Edition

Edited by Roger E. Axtell

Compiled by ✦ THE PARKER PEN COMPANY

with offices in 120 countries

A BENJAMIN BOOK

JOHN WILEY & SONS, INC.
New York • Chichester • Brisbane • Toronto • Singapore

Library of Congress Cataloging-in-Publication Data

Do's and taboos around the world / edited by Roger E. Axtell; compiled by the Parker Pen Company. — 3rd ed.
   208 p. 15 -1/4 x 22-3/4 cm
   "A Benjamin book."
   Includes bibliographical references and index.
   ISBN 0-471-59528-4 (Wiley)   0-87502-247-2 (Benjamin)
   1. Business etiquette. 2. Intercultural communication.
I. Axtell, Roger E. II. Parker Pen Company.
HF5387.D66 1993
395'.52—dc20   93-7558
                                        CIP

Illustrations by Robert Weber   Typography: Graphic Circle Inc.
                 Howard Munce

Cover Illustration by Robert Weber   Managing Editor: Virginia Schomp

Produced by The Benjamin Company, Inc.
            21 Dupont Avenue
            White Plains, NY 10605

Printed in the United States of America

12

Contents

OTHER BOOKS BY

ROGER E. AXTELL

The Do's and Taboos of International Trade, A Small Business, Primer, Wiley, 1991

The Do's and Taboos of Hosting InternationalVisitors, Wiley, 1990

GESTURES: The Do's and Taboos of Body Language Around the World, Wiley, 1991

Do's and Taboos of Public Speaking, How to Get Those Butterflies Flying in Formation, Wiley, 1992

Preface to
Third Edition

In July 1985 this book was launched via an interview on NBC's "Today" show. The national interest that followed brought a series of surprises.

Such interest astounded those who had compiled the book, because it had been created for what was thought to be a fairly limited audience, namely that small coterie of intrepid American businessmen and businesswomen who regularly venture abroad seeking new commerce.

Further, the book had been compiled and published by a seemingly unlikely source, The Parker Pen Company. For some ninety years Parker had accumulated substantial experience in selling its products overseas. Indeed, for the past fifty years Parker has been regarded as one of the best-known American brand names in the international marketplace - a fact few Americans realize even today.

So back in 1985 the people at Parker thought it might be helpful to share some of its specialized knowledge on dealing with people from other cultures. The Benjamin Company was asked to design and publish the book for Parker. A talented PR specialist, Ian Kerr, was hired to promote the book. And whamo! the surprises started rolling in, beginning with the "Today" show.

Soon after that interview stories appeared on the CNN network plus dozens of regional and local TV shows and on wire services including United Press, Associated Press, and Reuters. The editor was invited on TV shows hosted by Merv Griffin and Regis Philbin, and the *New Yorker* magazine dubbed him "the international Emily Post." Johnny Carson read excerpts on the "Tonight Show" and the book won a coveted national award from the Public Relations Society of America. The editor was invited to appear on ABC's "Good Morning America" TV show on three separate occasions.

In 1988 foreign-language publishers bought the rights to publish it in German, Japanese, and Finnish, plus two versions in French (one for Canada and one for France.)

When the book reached the 100,000 mark in 1990, a second edition was issued containing revisions and additions. Now this third edition is being released with even more updated and rewritten data to reflect changes around the world since 1985. For example, chapter 3 on "Gift Giving and Receiving" has been completely rewritten, and other segments in the book have been freshened because of monumental changes in Germany, the People's Republic of China, and other locales around the world.

Quite a success story. But, in truth, those who have labored over this book realize there is really only *one* reason why all this has been achieved. And that reason is that more and more readers have become sensitive to the need to communicate better in this shrinking world of ours. They have wanted to learn how to behave properly, avoid gaffes, eliminate embarrassments, and communicate more effectively with their shipmates on this so-called "spaceship earth."

In all three editions we have tried to present information to fill those needs with a lighthearted touch and tone. Our maxim: "Laughter has no accent." Such a message of universality is appropriate because, while this book lists hundreds of diverse cultural idiosyncrasies, it also says, "Everyone is ethnic ... yet we are all one."

ROGER E. AXTELL

Preface to
First Edition

It was the mid-1960s and the voice of Gamal Abdel Nasser issued from the radio while a fan waved slowly overhead. The house was large, white, and stucco, with marble floors providing some coolness.

Eight men were seated in a circle, some on overstuffed cushions, some on thick frieze chairs reminiscent of a Ginger Rogers movie.

Someone passed the wooden mouthpiece of the hookah, a water pipe with a long hose not unlike a vacuum cleaner hose. The hose was connected to a large bubbling beaker with tobacco burning in a bowl situated on top. The pipe was passed slowly around the room, mouth to mouth.

The group comprised seven brothers and one young and rather naive American businessman. The brothers all wore long Arab robes and were important customers. No women were in sight. No alcohol. And Nasser's emotional Arabic coming from the radio reminded the young American of the delicate politics hanging over the occasion. For someone born in Wisconsin, this was a most unfamiliar setting and an extremely important business occasion.

Two thoughts prevailed. First, avoid any social blunders in this most important moment. Second, get back to the hotel room and make notes on proper behavior and this extraordinary evening.

That vignette — the hookah, the robes, the need to make notes — was, perhaps, the origin of this book.

The need and opportunity for Americans to travel abroad are even stronger today than in the 1960s. And so is the need to avoid faux pas. More than ever the marketplace is global. Americans *must* move abroad, and move effectively, comfortably, and with the highest respect for other cultures.

The problem is that the rules for proper behavior are not very exact.

This book is *not* an anthropological study of *why* different peoples around the world behave in different ways. Instead, its purpose is to create an awareness of, or sensitivity to, behavior when one is traveling outside the United States or dealing in this country with a visitor from overseas. (Notice the word "foreigner" has been avoided? Who likes to be called a "foreigner"? We might label that as lesson number one.)

Ideally, this book will help each world traveler grow little invisible antennae that will sense incoming messages about cultural differences and nuances. An appreciation and understanding of these differences will prevent embarrassment, unhappiness, and failure. In fact, learning through travel about these cultural differences can be both challenging and fun.

This book is not — repeat, not — the definitive book on proper behavior. Some readers will say, "Oh, but that gesture or that practice may apply in the North of that country, but not in the South." And they may be right. This book is a compilation of surveys, research, and personal experiences in an area of study — human behavior — where there is never precise definition. You'll also find, because of our diverse sources, some variations in writing style.

Corrections, refinements, improvements, or additions are encouraged and welcomed. Send them to:

PJ Dempsey, Editor
John Wiley & Sons, Inc.
605 Third Avenue
New York, NY 10158

Roger E. Axtell

Acknowledgments

A compendium like this could not possibly be completed without the minds and hands of many people. The following alphabetical list acknowledges the contributions of those foremost among our contributors.

Brigham Young University's Center for International Area Studies is one of the few — and finest — resources available for the type of cultural information offered in this book. Such conscientious research and sensitivity to national behavior is a tribute to the evangelical work of the Mormon church.

Scott M. Cutlip had no direct involvement in this book. Instead, as the "grand seigneur" and dean of educators in public relations, he has instilled a profound responsibility within anyone who has practiced that craft since World War II. Coauthor of the first comprehensive textbook on public relations, he has been mentor, friend, and inspiration to the editor of this book.

Richard W. Holznecht was both supporter and contributor. He has a unique capability for nonconventional expression and his credo has been, when weaving words, strive for uniqueness and grace. He possesses that talent in unfair abundance.

Ian Kerr, Chairman, Kerr Kelly Inc., Greenwich, Connecticut, is a public relations consultant for major companies on both sides of the Atlantic. Born and educated in England, he has spent his career educating and serving clients in all forms of communications — with words and all other wisdom. He contributed large portions of both those commodities to this book.

George Parker is former Chairman of The Parker Pen Company. In 1902 his grandfather foresaw the need for American businessmen to travel and sell their products outside the U.S. During his tenure, George caused the greatest growth cycle in Parker's history and was responsible for sending Parker products and Parker travelers into every market of the world where hands hold writing instruments. His success in the tough field of consumer goods, competing against all nations, is an example to all in American business.

Cynthia Proulx and **Ian Keown** provided the finished writing for parts of the manuscript plus some additional research. Each has spent the last dozen or so years traveling far and wide and writing about it: Ian in frequent magazine features for *Travel & Leisure, Esquire,* and the airline magazines as well as in his own guidebooks *Caribbean Hideaways, Very Special Places,* and *European Hideaways;* Cynthia as a contributor to those guides and in her own magazine and newspaper articles.

Lois Puerner would have made one of the world's best mediators or negotiators because of her boundless patience, dedication, and pleasant disposition. Instead, she is only the finest secretary in the Western Hemisphere and silently suffered through surveys, rewrites, more rewrites, correspondence, and chaos. As the reader skips across the words in this volume in microseconds, pause occasionally in respect to the many times Mrs. Puerner struggled with each one.

Eugene G. Rohlman was Public Relations Manager of The Parker Pen Company and is the winner of numerous awards for writing, employee publications, and photography. This book would still be in its original womb - an overstuffed cardboard box - without the work and help of Gene Rohlman.

Virginia Schomp, formerly Vice President-Editorial Director of The Benjamin Company and now a free-lance writer and editor, has applied her highly professional editing skills to each of the three editions of this book. She provides accuracy, consistency, and readability — three essentials in a reference book such as this.

Nina Streitfeld, formerly a Vice President of Kerr Kelly Inc., serves as President of Nina Streitfeld, Inc., a public relations firm with national and international clients, and is currently a member of the Board of Directors of the Tri-State American-Japanese Society. With the help of Research Assistant Sherry Ek, Nina was responsible for the survey and research in this book's "American Jargon" section.

Robert R. Williams is a bright, witty, and intelligent public relations resource (Idea Associates, Stevens Point, Wisconsin) who provided encouragement and ideas for this volume.

CHAPTER 1

Protocol, Customs, and Etiquette

Three Great Gaffes
or
One country's good manners, another's grand faux pas

In Washington they call protocol "etiquette with a government expense account." But diplomacy isn't just for diplomats. How you behave in other people's countries reflects on more than you alone. It also brightens — or dims — the image of where you come from and whom you work for. The Ugly American about whom we used to read so much may be dead, but here and there the ghost still wobbles out of the closet.

Three well-traveled Americans tell how even an old pro can sometimes make the wrong move in the wrong place at the wrong time.

A partner in one of New York's leading private banking firms

When the board chairman is Lo Win Hao, do you smile brightly and say, "How do you do, Mr. Hao?" or "Mr. Lo"? Or "Mr. Win"?

"I traveled nine thousand miles to meet a client and arrived with my foot in my mouth. Determined to do things right, I'd memorized the names of the key men I was to see in Singapore. No easy job, inasmuch as the names all came in threes. So, of course, I couldn't resist showing off that I'd done my homework. I began by addressing top man Lo Win Hao with plenty of well-placed Mr. Hao's — and sprinkled the rest of my remarks with a Mr. Chee this and a Mr. Woon that. Great show. Until a note was passed to me from one man I'd met before, in New York. Bad news. 'Too friendly too soon, Mr. Long,' it said. Where diffidence is next to godliness, there I was, calling a roomful of VIP's, in effect, Mr. Ed and Mr. Charlie. I'd remembered everybody's name — but forgotten that in Chinese the surname comes *first* and the given name *last*."

An associate in charge of family planning for an international human welfare organization

The lady steps out in her dazzling new necklace and everybody dies laughing. (Or what not to wear in Togo on a Saturday night.)

"From growing up in Cuba to joining the Peace Corps to my present work, I've spent most of my life in the Third World. So nobody should know better than I how to dress for it. Certainly one of the silliest mistakes an outsider can make is to dress up in 'native' costume, whether it's a sari or a sombrero, unless you really know what you're doing. Yet, in Togo, when I found some of the most beautiful beads I'd ever seen, it never occurred to me not to wear them. While I was up-country, I seized the first grand occasion to flaunt my new find. What I didn't know is that locally the beads are worn not at the neck but at the waist — to hold up a sort of loincloth under the skirt. So, into the party I strutted, wearing around my neck what to every Togolese eye was part of a pair of underpants."

An account executive at an international data processing and electronics conglomerate

Even in a country run by generals, would you believe a runny nose could get you arrested?

"A friend and I were coming into Colombia on business after a weekend in the Peruvian mountains touring Machu Picchu. What a sight that had been. And what a head cold the change in temperature had given my friend. As we proceeded through Customs at the airport, he was wheezing and blowing into his handkerchief like an active volcano. Next thing I knew, two armed guards were lockstepping him through a door. I tried to intercede before the door slammed shut, but my spotty Spanish failed me completely. Inside a windowless room with the guards, so did his. He shouted in English. They shouted in Spanish. It was beginning to look like a bad day in Bogotá when a Colombian woman who had seen what happened burst into the room and finally achieved some bilingual understanding. It seems all that sniffling in the land of the infamous coca leaf had convinced the guards that my friend was waltzing through their airport snorting cocaine."

Cuddly Ethnocentrics

If only the world's Customs inspectors could train their German shepherds to sniff out the invisible baggage we all manage to slip with us into foreign countries. They are like secret little land mines of the mind. Set to go off at the slightest quiver, they can sabotage a five-minute stroll down the Champs-Élysées or a $5,000,000 tractor sale to Beijing. Three of our most popular national take-alongs:

Why Don't They Speak English? For the same reason we don't speak Catalan or Urdu. The wonder, in fact, is that so many people do speak so many languages. Seldom is a Continental European fluent in fewer than three, often more. Africans grow up with the language of the nation that once colonized theirs plus half a dozen different tribal dialects. Japan has three distinct Japanese languages, which even the lowliest street sweeper can understand. Middle Eastern businesspeople shift effortlessly from their native tongue(s) to Oxford English to Quai d'Orsay French. Yet most of the English-speaking world remains as cheerfully monolingual as Queen Victoria's parakeet. If there are any complaints, then, it is clear they should not be coming from the American/English-speaking traveler.

Take Me to Your Burger King. In Peoria a Parisian does not go looking for pot-au-feu. Alone among travelers, Americans seem to embark like astronauts — sealed inside a cozy life-support system from home. Scrambled eggs. Rent-a-cars. Showers. TV. Nothing wrong with any of it back home, but to the rest of the universe it looks sadly like somebody trying to read a book with the cover closed. Experiment! Try the local specialties.

American Know-How to the Rescue! Our brightest ideas have taken root all over the world — from assembly lines in Düsseldorf to silicon chips in Osaka to hybrid grains that are helping to nourish the Third World. Nonetheless, bigger, smarter, and faster do not inevitably add up to better. Indeed, the desire to take on shiny new American ways has been the downfall of nations whose cultures were already rich in art and technology when North America was still a glacier. As important as the idea itself is the way it is presented.

A U.S. doctor of public health recently back from West Africa offers an example of how to make the idea fit the ideology. "I don't just pop over and start handing out antimalarial pills on the corner," she says. "First I visit with the village chief. After he gives his blessing, I move in with the local witch doctor. After she shows me her techniques and I show her mine — and a few lives are saved — maybe then we can get the first native to swallow the first pill."

This is as true at the high-tech level as at the village dispensary. "What is all this drinking of green tea before the meeting with Mitsubishi?" The American way is to get right down to business. Yet if you look at Mitsubishi's bottom line, you have to wonder if green tea is such a bad idea after all.

It should come as no surprise that people surrounded by oceans rather than by other people end up ethnocentric. Even our biggest fans admit that America often strikes the rest of the world as a sweet-but-spoiled little darling, wanting desperately,

5

to please but not paying too much attention to how it is done. Ever since the Marshall Plan, we seemed to believe that *our* games and *our* rules were the only ones in town. Any town. And that all else was the Heart of Darkness.

Take this scene in a Chinese cemetery. Watching a Chinese reverently placing fresh fruit on a grave, an American visitor asked, "When do you expect your ancestors to get up and eat the fruit?" The Chinese replied, "As soon as your ancestors get up and smell the flowers."

Hands Across the Abyss

Our bad old habits are giving way to a new when-in Rome awareness. Some corporations take it so seriously that they put employees into a crash course of overseas cultural immersion. AT&T, for instance, encourages — and pays for — the whole family of an executive on the way to a foreign assignment to enroll in classes given by experts in the mores and manners of other lands.

Among the areas that cry out loudest for international understanding are how to say people's names, eat, dress, and talk. Get those four basics right and the rest is a piece of kuchen.

Basic Rule #1: What's in a name?

Good-bye, Notowidigeo. Hello. Sastroamidjojo. At the U.S. State Department, foreign names are almost as crucial as foreign policy. The social secretary to a former secretary of state recalls that even in the relatively unselfconscious 1950s, she put herself through a rigorous rehearsal of names before every affair of state. Of all the challenges, she says, the ambassador from what was then Ceylon (now Sri Lanka) was the toughest. After days of practicing "Ambassador Notowidigeo," she was informed that a new man had the job — and was on his way to be received. "You'd be surprised how fast you can memorize Sastroamidjojo when you have to," she adds.

The first transaction between even ordinary citizens — and the first chance to make an impression for better or worse — is, of course, an exchange of names. In America there usually is not very much to get wrong. And even if you do, so what?

Not so elsewhere. Especially in the Eastern Hemisphere, where name frequently denotes social rank or family status, a mistake can be an outright insult. So can switching to a given name without the other person's permission, even when you think the situation calls for it.

"What would you like me to call you?" is always the opening line of one overseas deputy director for an international telecommunications corporation. "Better to ask several times," he advises, "than to get it wrong." Even then, "I err on the side of formality until asked to 'Call me Joe'." Another frequent traveler insists his company provide him with a list of key people he will meet, country by country, surnames underlined, to be memorized on the flight over.

Don't trust the rules

Just when you think you have broken the international name code, they switch the rules on you. Take Latin America. Most people's names are a combination of the father's and mother's, with only the father's name used in conversation. In the Spanish-speaking countries the father's name comes first. Hence, Carlos Mendoza-Miller is called Mr. Mendoza. *But* in Portuguese-speaking Brazil it is the other way around, with the mother's name first.

In the Orient the Chinese system of surname first, given name last does not always apply. The Taiwanese, many of whom were educated in missionary schools, often have a Christian first name, which comes before any of the others — as in Tommy Ho Chin, who should be called Mr. Ho or, to his friends, Tommy Ho. Also, given names are often officially changed to initials, and a Y.Y. Lang is Y.Y.; never mind what it stands for. In Korea, which of a man's names takes a Mr. is determined by whether he is his father's first or second son. Although in Thailand names run backwards, Chinese style, the Mr. is put with the *given* name, and to a Thai it is just as important to be called by his given name as it is for a Japanese to be addressed by his surname. With the latter, incidentally, you can in a very friendly relationship respond to his using *your* first name by dropping the Mr. and adding *san* to his last name, as in Ishikawa-san.

Hello. Are you still there? Then get ready for the last installment of the name game, which is to disregard all of the above — sometimes. The reason is that many Easterners who deal regularly with the West are now changing the order of their names to un-confuse us. So, while to one another their names remain the same, to us the given name may come before the surname. Then again, it may not.

The safest course remains: ask.

Don't Leave Home Without It

Overseas the ultimate passport is the business card — proof that you really do exist. Even a casual exchange of names between tourist and native usually calls for it. Any business contact demands it. Not just because, to a foreigner, your name is foreign and hence easier to absorb in writing, but particularly because rank and profession are taken so much more seriously than here at home. A reporter, for instance, is never called a mere reporter but a *journalist*, with the lofty implications of a James Reston or Walter Cronkite. In Italy even a bachelor's degree entitles you to put a *Dr.* in front of your name. *Professor* is also used much more loosely than in the U.S. In Asia it is not so much *who* you are as *where* you are in the pecking order of any given meeting or transaction. Suggestions:

- On the card include your company name and your position plus any titles such as vice president, manager, associate director. Don't use abbreviations.

- If you are going where English is not widely spoken, take your cards to a printer when you get there and have the reverse side printed in the local language. (In Hong Kong and Tokyo, overnight service is available.)

- In most of Southeast Asia, Africa, and the Middle East (except Israel), never present the card with your left hand.

- In Japan present it with both hands, and make sure the type is facing the recipient and is right side up.

Basic Rule #2: Eat, drink, and be wary.

Pass the gorilla, please. Away from home, eating is more than just a way to keep your pin-striped suit from falling off. It is a language all its own, and no words can match it for saying "Glad to meet you . . . glad to be doing business with you . . . glad to have you here in the beautiful Rann of Kutch" or wherever.

Clearly, mealtime is no time for a thanks-but-no-thanks response. Acceptance of what is on your plate is tantamount to acceptance of host, country, and company. So, no matter how tough things may be to swallow, swallow. Or, as one veteran globe-girdler puts it, "Travel with a cast-iron stomach and eat everything everywhere."

Tastiness is in the eye of the beholder

Often, what is offered constitutes your host country's proudest culinary achievements. What would we Americans think of a Frenchman who refused a bite of homemade apple pie or sizzling sirloin? Squeamishness comes not so much from the thing itself as from our unfamiliarity with it. After all, an oyster has remarkably the same look and consistency as a sheep's eye, and at first encounter a lobster would strike almost anybody as more a creature from science fiction than something you dip in melted butter and pop into your mouth.

Incidentally, in Saudi Arabia sheep's eyes are a delicacy, and in China it's bear's paw soup.

Perhaps the ultimate in exotic dining abroad befell a family planning expert on a trip for an international human welfare organization. It was a newly emerged African country where the national dish — in fact, the *only* dish eleven months of the year — is yam. The visitor's luck, however, was to be there the *other* month, when gorillas come in from the bush to steal the harvest. Being the only available protein, gorilla meat is as prized as sirloin is over here, and the village guest of honor was served a choice cut. Proudly, a platter of the usual mashed yams was placed before her — but with a roast gorilla hand thrusting artfully up from the center.

Is there any polite way out besides the back door?

Most experienced business travelers say no, at least not before taking at least a few bites. It helps, though, to slice whatever the item is very thin. This way, you minimize the texture — gristly, slimy, etc. — and the reminder of whence it came. Or, "Swallow it quickly," as one traveler recommends. "I still can't tell you what sheep's eyeballs taste like." As for dealing with taste, the old canard that "it tastes just like chicken" is often mercifully true. Even when the "it" is rodent, snake — or gorilla.

Another useful dodge is not knowing what you are eating. What's for dinner? Don't ask. Avoid poking around in the kitchen or looking at English-language menus. Your host will be flattered that you are following his lead, and who knows? Maybe it really is chicken in that stew.

Will you pasta the test?

In Europe the hazard is not so much exotica as richness, amplitude, and hour. In Italy and Spain (as well as in Latin America), lunch is the biggest meal of the day and can last two or three hours. Work nevertheless is expected to continue afterward. Because Latins are used to this regimen — and wisely eat a very light breakfast and late-late supper — it does not mean the rest of us can take on a seven-course lunch, *con vino*, and survive a 4:30 meeting. If food is served family style from communal dishes, take just a little of everything. When ordering from the menu, ask for appetizer portions instead of entrée size, especially of the heavier pasta dishes. In French restaurants request that, if possible, sauces be served on the side. In Scandinavia do not try matching your host's trips around the smorgasbord herring for herring. Another trick is to order two appetizers, the second appetizer becoming your entrée; that way you eat sparingly but are politely eating in pace with your hosts.

Speaking of fish, in Japan it is often served raw. Nearly every meal begins with it and some restaurants serve nothing but. Although sushi bars may be just as trendy here as there, many Americans still find raw *any*thing literally tough going.

Sushi (a circle of raw fish packed artfully in rice) and sashimi (same thing without rice) are a problem for the uninitiated because they cannot be cut into small bites — it is all in one gulp or nothing. But there is usually red caviar sushi and sometimes Japanese vegetables can be substituted. One worldly Swiss who thought he had seen — and eaten — just about everything in the Orient describes, not so fondly, how he temporarily lost his taste for fish there. At a lavish Tokyo restaurant, delicacy after delicacy had been served. Then the pièce de résistance. A live fish was brought flopping and gasping to the table and was delicately sliced by the maitre d' and served a piece at a time.

How to say no in Chinese

In Chinese cultures (Taiwan, Hong Kong, and Singapore as well as the mainland), the trick is to say it with*out* saying it. An endless history of famine and deprivation has made it bad manners for the host not to keep filling your dish — and for you not to keep eating as long as your dish is full. Obviously, a no-win situation.

(Incidentally, it is not rude for the Chinese to use the chopsticks they eat with to serve you.)

Eat what you are offered.

One way to discourage refills is to keep your rice bowl close to your mouth until you are done. Then lay your chopsticks across the bowl to signify "enough!" However, you will probably have more than one dish, thus undermining the effectiveness of the chopstick ploy. Same for your teacup, which seems to be magically replenishing itself no matter how much you drink. To stop the flow, leave your cup full. To say thank you, rap your fingertips lightly on the table. And always leave some food in your dish to indicate that your host was so generous you could not possibly finish.

Shark's fin soup is often the highlight of a Chinese multicourse dinner, served somewhere in the middle, and — incidentally — the polite time for toast making. Also, the second-to-last course is often plain boiled rice — which you should refuse! To eat it signifies you are still hungry and is an insult to the host.

Menus by Dostoevsky

In Russia it is not unusual to find restaurants closed to *every*one at lunchtime. The help, you see, are out to lunch. But even when they are on the job, there may be a classic Russian wait — as long as two hours before a waiter or waitress gives you a sidelong glance. Be consoled, though. You always have at your table two large bottles — one of mineral water, the other of 100-proof vodka. Provided you can still read by the time the waiter gets there, you will find the menu an adventure all its own. "Every Continental dish ever served from Saint Petersburg to Sicily is listed," reports a New Yorker back from Moscow. With a red plush cover, golden tassels, and nearly as many words as *War and Peace,* this is austerity?

In theory, no. But then you order. Nyet. Nyet. Nyet. That is your waiter advising you that they do not have that tonight . . . or that . . . or that. Until you give up and ask what they *do* have. The answer varies. In some restaurants it is fish, in others chicken. So you turn to page 42 of your menu, marked "Chicken." More nyets. Okay, *which* chicken? Chicken Kiev, of course. Henry Ford, who promised to give American consumers any color car they wanted as long as it was black, would have approved.

And then there are Russian breakfasts, alas not designed to appease appetites weaned on flapjacks and sunny-sides. The usual choice is compressed fish (a layer cake of whatever turns up in the net, flash-frozen and then more or less thawed) and/or hard-boiled eggs. One visitor exultantly discovered a big, juicy Danish pastry in his hotel cafeteria one morning on his last trip, It took just one bite to reveal that it was more Russian than Danish, however, being stuffed with raw cabbage.

But be consoled: New restaurants and hotels are springing up in many of the major cities of the former Soviet Union. Prices are often high, but the new establishments offer Western-style luxuries seldom found on the traditional Russian menu.

Table Talk

THANK-YOU'S*		**TOASTS***
Shay-shay	Mandarin	Kam-*pay*
Doe-jay	Cantonese	Yum-*sing*
Arr-i-gah-*toe*	Japanese	Kam-*pai*
Shu-kran	Arabic	No alcohol, no toast
Grah-see-as	Spanish	Sah-*lood*
Ohb-ri-*gah*-toe	Portuguese	Sah-*ude*
Grahtz-ee	Italian	Sah-*loo*-tay
Mare-*see*	French	Ah-votre-sahn-*tay*
Dahnk-ah	German	*Pro*-zit
Tak	Scandinavian	Skoal
Spa-see-*bow*	Russian	Nah-zda-*roe*-vee-ah

*Phonetic spellings

Also, while Americans answer a "thank-you" with a "you're welcome," the English don't. They answer a "thank-you" with a "thank-you."

Bottoms up — or down?

Some countries seem to do it deliberately, some inadvertently, except for Islam, where they don't do it at all. Either way, getting visitors as tipsy as possible as fast as possible stands as a universal sign of hospitality, and refusal to play your part equals rebuff. Wherever you go, toasts are as reciprocal as handshakes: if one does, all do. "I don't drink, thank you" rarely gets you off gracefully. Neither does protesting that you must get up early. (So must everyone else.)

"I try to wangle a glass of wine instead of the local firewater," one itinerant American says. "The only trouble is, the wine is usually stronger than the hard stuff." Mao-tai,

Chinese wine made from sorghum, is notorious for leaving the unsuspecting thoroughly shanghaied. The Georgian wine so popular in Russia is no ladylike little Chablis either. In Nordic lands proper form for the toast is to raise the glass in a sweeping arc from belt buckle to lips while locking stares with your host. It takes very few akvavit-with-beer-chasers before you both start seeing northern lights.

In Africa, where all the new countries were once old European colonies, it is often taken for granted that if you are white you must have whiskey or gin or whatever the colonials used to like. A traveler to a former French possession describes the dilemma of being served a large gourdful of Johnnie Walker Red at nine in the morning. The host was simply remembering how the French had always loved their Scotch. *When* they drank it and *how much* were details he had never noticed. Yet there was no saying no without giving offense. A few sips had to be taken and a promise made to finish the rest later.

Basic Rule #3: Clothes can also *un*make the man.

Black tie, green tails. It was a very proper black-tie affair in Australia's capital of Canberra. In a sea of ebony dinner jackets and starchy white shirtfronts bobbed a small riot of color — namely, the U.S. ambassador clad in dazzling pea green sports coat and multihued plaid trousers. Why, the ambassador's wife asked plaintively, do these Aussies gape at us every time we show up at one of their fancy-dress receptions?

Wherever you are, what you wear among strangers should not look strange to *them*. Which does not mean, "When in Morocco wear djellabas," etc. It means wear what you look natural in — and know how to wear — that also fits in with your surroundings.

For example, a woman dressed in a tailored suit, even with high heels and flowery blouse, looks startlingly masculine in a country full of diaphanous saris. More appropriate, then, is a silky, loose-fitting dress in a bright color — as opposed to blue serge or banker's gray.

In downtown Nairobi, a safari jacket looks as out of place as in London. With a few exceptions (where the weather is just too steamy for it), the general rule everywhere is that for business, for eating out, even for visiting people at home, you should be very buttoned up: conservative suit and tie for men, dress or skirt-suit for women. To be left in the closet until you go on an outdoor sight-seeing trek:

- jeans, however haute couture
- jogging shoes
- tennis and T-shirts
- tight-fitting sweaters (women)
- open-to-the-navel shirts (men)
- funny hats (both)

Where you *can* loosen up, it is best to do it the way the indigenes do. In the Philippines men wear the barong tagalog — a loose, frilly, usually white or cream-colored shirt with tails out, no jacket or tie. In tropical Latin American countries the counterpart to the barong is called a *guayabera* and, except for formal occasions, is acceptable business attire. In Indonesia they wear *batiks* — brightly patterned shirts that go tieless and jacketless everywhere. In Thailand the same is true for the collarless Thai silk shirt. In Japan dress is at least as formal as in Europe (dark suit and tie for a man, business suit or tailored dress for a woman) except at country inns (called *ryokans*), where even big-city corporations sometimes hold meetings. Here you are expected to wear a kimono. Not to daytime meetings but to dinner, no matter how formal. (Don't worry — the inn always provides the kimono.)

One thing you notice wherever you go is that polyester is the mark of the tourist. The less drip-dry you are, the more you look as if you have come to do serious business, even if it means multiple dry-cleaning bills along the way.

Take it off or put it on — depending

What you do or do not wear can be worse than bad taste — ranging from insulting to unhygienic to positively sinful. Shoes are among the biggest offenders in the East, even if you wear a 5AAA. They are forbidden within Muslim mosques and Buddhist temples. Never wear them into Japanese homes or restaurants unless the owner insists, and in Indian and Indonesian homes, if the host goes shoeless, do likewise. And wherever you take your shoes off, remember to place them neatly together facing the door you came in. This is particularly important in Japan.

15

(Note: The torture of sitting for hours cross-legged on tatami mats has been alleviated lately in some Japanese restaurants, which have thoughtfully cut a hole in the floor under the table so Westerners can unfold their legs.)

In certain conservative Arab countries, the price for wearing the wrong thing can hurt more than feelings. Mullahs have been known to give a sharp whack with their walking sticks to any woman whom they consider immodestly dressed. Even at American-style hotels there, do not wear shorts, skirts above the knee, sleeveless blouses, or low necklines — much less a bikini at the pool.

Basic Rule #4: American spoken here. You hope.

It is nice to be born free. But we should be just as grateful that we were also born speaking the language more people speak besides their own than any other. Even where Americans aren't understood, American is. It is when we try to talk in other tongues that the most dramatic failures of communication seem to occur.

At a party in Bernardsville, New Jersey. A high-level U.S. communications man invited a group of visiting Taiwanese whom he had met in Taiwan to a reception at his house. He also invited some neighbors, one of whom had the bright idea of asking her laundryman how to say hello in Chinese. He gave her the words—but not the warning that every Chinese word has many meanings, depending on the tone you use. As the first Taiwanese came in the door, she delivered a smart "How do you do?" in Chinese. Bewildered, the guest turned to the host and demanded, "Why is this woman talking about my mother?" The word to indicate a question also means horse and scold and sesame seed—and mother. A case of wrong tone, wrong meaning.

At a banquet in Beijing. As the honored guests at one of China's famous twelve-course governmental dinners, a delegation of heavy-duty equipment manufacturers from the Midwest had just laid down their chopsticks. It was time for a word, in quickly memorized phonetic Chinese, from our side. "Thank you very much for the dinner. I am so full I must loosen my belt" is the toast the Americans had prepared. But through the vagaries of the language what was actually delivered was, "The girth of thy donkey's saddle is loose." Again, good thought, bad pronunciation.

Sometimes the way we speak is as misinterpreted as what we are trying to say. Take the "conversation tango" we are accused of dancing with Latins. Most of us prefer to keep our distance in casual conversation — two or three feet apart when face-to-face. Nearly every South American, however, feels positively lonely at such a remove. He immediately tries to establish intimacy and intensity by virtually nose-to-nosing it with you. You take a step back, he takes a step forward. Back . . . forward . . . back . . . forward. Cha-cha-cha. Trouble is, the net impression can be: 1) you are a snob or 2) he is not nice to be near. The embarrassment to both sides is not worth demanding your territorial rights. So stand your ground and let him stand his.

English English

"England and America," George Bernard Shaw said, "are divided by a common language." To an American on London's Carnaby Street, English English can sound as foreign as Brooklynese to a member of the House of Lords.

Fridge, loo, telly, wireless, and chemist's are all easy enough to decipher. But who would suspect that a bonnet is a car hood, a vest an undershirt, a panda a police car, a counter jumper a salesman — or fanny an X-rated word (use bum instead)? Should you run into a serious cockney, one who drops his aitches and substitutes rhyming phrases for words (trouble-and-strife for wife), you may as well be talking in Minsk.

Belgium has two official languages, Dutch and French, and the character of the country changes with the language. Around Antwerp (where there are mostly Flemish and hence Dutch), you find more order and efficiency in the way things get done. Around Brussels (where there are mostly Walloons and hence French), you find more three-star restaurants. A nice contrast, either way.

Never-never land

It is a basic precept of Japanese culture that the best face must be put on even the worst situation — which sounds comforting but can have confusing consequences. For a Westerner given to firm yes's and no's, either it *is* a deal or it isn't. For his Japanese counterpart, a smile, a nod, even a spoken affirmative can simply be reluctance to disappoint — especially in front of others.

Ask the man in charge for an answer to your business proposition and not only will he be offended but his answer will be meaningless. Those details are expected to have been disposed of at a lower level, privately, between subalterns.

Unfortunately, when you are asking a cabdriver if he understands where you want to go, there is no one else to answer for him. Nine times out of ten, he will indicate "you bet!" and step on the gas. Many visitors to the Ginza have, as a result, found themselves in Osaka. One man of the world thought he had solved the problem. When leaving his hotel, he would have the concierge write out his destination in Japanese characters. For his return, he would simply take a hotel matchbook and flash it at the driver. Late one night, he discovered that the matchbook has its drawbacks.

As usual, the driver took one look and zoomed purposefully off. The ride had begun to seem unusually long, however, and downtown Tokyo was nowhere in sight when the cab stopped. All was empty streets and darkened warehouses. The driver had taken him not to the Okura Hotel but to the matchbook factory.

If you ever do hear a no in Japan, from either cabdriver or captain of industry, it is likely to be not so much a word as a sucking of breath through the teeth that comes out sounding like "sah." Otherwise, the closest anyone comes is to say sadly, "It is very difficult."

Tread softly and carry a dictionary

Some languages cannot be understood as pronounced by outsiders. But no matter how you twist most native tongues some meaning gets through — or at least you get an *A* for effort if it doesn't. Memorizing a toast or greeting (in spite of the tales above) nearly always serves to break the ice, if not the communications barrier.

Even in France, where abusing the language is as punishable as stomping the tricolor, you find that to take out an English-French dictionary nearly always draws a crowd avid to help you unravel the mysteries of how to say, "Where is the Metro, please?"

But no matter how fluently the natives speak your language, remember that it is never spoken — or understood — quite the same way it is at home. Steer clear of all slanguage, from colloquialisms to curses to down-home references that have about as much resonance in Paris or Beijing as grits and chitlins.

This is especially true if you are reaching your audience through a translator. Deliberately or not, what *he* is telling them

may not be what *you* are telling them. One company spokesman from Wisconsin, using an interpreter at an overseas press conference, found that his message had been completely misunderstood. Not through mischief, but because the interpreter had added a touch of glamour and newsworthiness to what struck him as deadly dull business talk. Whenever possible, have another bilingual there to monitor the translation for you so you know what you really said.

George Washington? Who's he?

That is no way for a foreigner to win friends in Washington. Nor is arriving on someone else's doorstep knowing nothing of the government, economics, religion, history, or national character of the place the way for an American to hit a home run. Yet those harried business trips with their if-it's-Tuesday-this-must-be-Zagreb itineraries can leave anyone speechless.

If you can possibly schedule a lunch with a couple of people who have lived or done a lot of business where you are going, it will be well worth the price of a fillet of sole. Also, grab the last few issues of a newsmagazine if your destination is often in the news. This way, even if you do not have any real background on it, you will at least be able to discuss what happened there last week.

If your company has a library, you can get a cram course right out of the files. Or, if you have branches in the places where you are headed, write ahead asking for a briefing. Whatever you get in return will at least be enough to start asking intelligent questions when you get there. Instead of "Mobutu? Who's he?"

Talking business

When you *don't* talk business can be as important as when you *do*. In Britain, for instance, as soon as the day is done, so is business, and nothing will turn your hosts off faster than continuing shoptalk over drinks and dinner.

On the other hand, to the Japanese there is almost no distinction between the business day and the business night. They consider it part of both their personal and professional lives to spend virtually every evening with business associates. Not at the office but at bars, nightclubs, geisha houses, and private clubs. Whether business is or is not discussed, the purpose is nonetheless business. "You get through to a man's soul at night" is a saying among Japanese businessmen. No matter how many mornings you have ended the business day at 4 A.M., begging off is bad form.

One time when you do *not* talk business in Japan, though, is at the beginning of first meetings. Introductions call for a set ritual. Business cards are exchanged. Tea is poured. And then more tea is poured. And still more. However anxious you are to get started, this is a not-to-be-rushed first step that the Japanese use to digest not just the tea but who you are, where you fit into your company's pecking order, and how your status relates to their status. This information about you is passed among those present — as well as to people not even in the room — so your counterparts can agree precisely on how to deal with you.

The same slow, analytical start often occurs in Arab countries, too. But with an added dimension: the multiple meeting. While conducting business with you in his office, the man in charge is very likely talking to a stream of other people wandering in and out. You may be dropped in midsentence and not picked up again for twenty minutes. No disrespect is meant; this is the communal "family style" in which Middle Eastern business is done. Do not be surprised, then, when a meeting you thought would take an hour takes two or three. And do not go over someone's head because you think there is a faster way to get a quick decision. It has the opposite effect.

Religion and Sex: Protocol at Its Pinnacle

If discussing politics is like playing with matches, transgressions in the areas of religion and sex are like playing with live hand grenades. Still, neither area can be ignored. Religion is often an important part of a culture (e.g., the Middle East) and therefore an unavoidable adjunct to business or tourist travel. For Westerners, who are usually Christian-oriented, a respectful — repeat, respectful — conversation about some of the other great religions of the world can be both illuminating and ingratiating.

As for sex, while Americans are slowly learning to change their vocabulary from *businessman* to *businessperson*, that change is not occurring as rapidly outside the U.S. In most other countries *business* is still largely synonymous with *men*.

Thus, both subjects should be dealt with head-on. Here goes.

Where religion is a religion

When a prosperous international advertising agency opened an office in Bangkok, the manager was warned it would never succeed. But why not? All the agency's other Far Eastern branches were having great success. "Ah," it was explained, "you never put yourself above Buddha before!" (A prominent statue of the god was, in fact, one flight below the new office and just across the street.) After a year there, business was still zero. In spite of himself, the manager decided to be philosophical about it and moved the office to where there was no Buddha, and business has been thriving evern since.

All Buddhist images, even the famous tourist sites, are holy and never to be photographed without permission. Other Thai sensitivities lurk where you would never expect to find them. Doorsills must never be stepped on, for Thais believe that kindly spirits dwell below. But to open a window at night is to let evil spirits in. And to touch the head of even a close friend risks ending the friendship, so sacred do they consider the head.

In Hong Kong the key word is *joss*, which loosely translated means good luck but is more akin to a blessing.

In Muslim countries, proper dress and proper decorum between the sexes are as important as observing any civil laws. It is no mere quaint local custom to stop everything five times a day for prayers. While you are not expected to kneel or face Mecca, you must let those who do do — without interruption or impatience. Whenever it can be done gracefully, making a religious gesture toward an Arab is the sincerest form of flattery. It can be as simple as saying *Inshallah*, which means "God willing" and is used as commonly as "okay" is here. As in "See you tomorrow, *Inshallah*," or "When does your flight leave, *Inshallah?*" It is easy to pick up the habit—and a nice compliment to your host.

Also remember that every culture has its own holidays, which are considered truly *holy days*. To schedule a business trip during Ramadan, Carnival in Rio, Chinese New Year, etc., is like a foreigner's asking you to attend a meeting on Christmas morning. For the holidays and their dates, contact the consulate or tourist bureau or check with a travel agent.

In the battle of the sexes, America is still way ahead

From mailrooms to boardrooms, women are becoming as commonplace in American corridors of power as button-downs

Don't photograph religious images.

and wing tips. Here but not there. Around most of the world, it is the same old *Vive la différence.*

In Britain and Western Europe a few women have risen — or are rising — through the ranks. Nevertheless, at every level above bookkeeper and clerk you will be dealing with a solid phalanx of homburgs and bowlers. Usually, there is no awkwardness when a Ms. VIP sits down at the conference table. And she will suffer no embarrassment eating alone in restaurants or even stopping off for a drink at a pub or bistro. (The latter is not quite so true, though, in Spain, Portugal, Southern Italy, and Greece.)

The farther east you go, the tougher the going gets. A New York banker reports that just a dozen years ago she was refused a visa to parts of the Middle East on the grounds that she was both a woman and single. Even today women are forbidden to drive cars or ride bicycles in Saudi Arabia.

Another American, invited to the wedding party for the daughter of a close Arab friend, discovered that separate is equal but still very separate. The party was actually *two* parties at two different hotels, each with exactly the same banquet and exactly the same festivities. The only difference was that one was for the bride and all the female guests, while the other was for the groom and all the male guests. Never the twain did meet.

Even if an Arab invites you home, his wife (or wives) will probably not be seen (although she may well be in the kitchen supervising dinner). It is not polite to inquire about her (them), and if you do meet, be warm but undemonstrative. Do not even shake hands unless she takes the initiative, which she no doubt will not. On the other hand, when the same Arab businessman comes to your country, his wife just may accompany him and then she should receive all the courtesies of any Western woman.

Whether you are a man or a woman, it is advisable to mention your family life as assurance of your stability as a business associate. In Eastern cultures family ties are extremely important, and for those who come from a less family-oriented part of the world, it does not hurt to refer to hearth and home. Of course, replays of Little League games and snapshots of the barbecue and the hamster can put anyone to sleep.

Sorry, ladies — no wrestling or geishas

The one place of business in Japan where women can be found in large numbers and at high levels is the geisha house. Ironically, women guests are not welcome, however. (Not because geisha houses are bordellos. They are not. But because the "girls" consider it their territory.) When a U.S. financial manager insisted his wife accompany him, she received a stern lecture from the English-speaking geisha at their table. The American, she said, was "a good woman, clever with children" and therefore belonged at home with them — not out on the town, sipping sake and listening to samisen music.

In case you might be feeling athletic, two other men-only spots in Japan are sumo wrestling rings and certain mountains considered too sacred to be climbed by women, who are also forbidden to touch Buddhist priests or even hand them anything except through an intermediary (male, of course).

Lecturer and writer Anna Chennault, a business consultant on the Orient, declared, "Chinese women do not worry about liberation. They have been liberated because of necessity." Perhaps, but few women are noticeable in the upper reaches of the People's Republic's officialdom, although they do comprise 60 percent of the labor force. But in the Philippines women seem to be in charge of many things. Filipino families educate their daughters in U.S. universities — and not necessarily to be wives, but also bankers and lawyers.

Women also have a very strong role in Africa, both in the home and in business. Yet visitors should remember that in Muslim — and Buddhist — nations, the religious stricture against mixing the sexes socially still obtains. A woman traveling as chief emissary for her Fortune 500 corporation was surprised after meeting with men all day to be placed at a table with their wives at dinner. The wife of the chairman emeritus of a multinational advertising agency has found this to be an advantage. After countless tours of her husband's worldwide advertising empire, she says she learns more about the country *and* the company from the wives. Their eye for detail, their slight remove from office politics, and their candor bring a different perspective to the conversation. And when an office manager won't admit to a problem or to a daring idea, often his wife will admit it for him.

In Latin America as well, women are smoothly accepted into business and governmental hierarchies. But in a land where machismo is every man's birthright, it does not pay to come on like Superwoman.

At presentations, sales meetings, even in personal conversations — particularly when the woman speaking outranks any men present— it is useful to avoid a lot of "I did"s and "I know"s in favor of "At our company we found that..." or "We approach the problem this way ...." Not bad advice for men, either.

After-hours etiquette

Never risk losing your credentials as a serious businesswoman by what you do *after* business. In Western European countries this is almost never an issue. But elsewhere it is easy to raise eyebrows — and lower your prestige. It isn't so much what you actually do as what it *looks* as if you might do.

1. Avoid eating or drinking alone in restaurants that the locals or business travelers use to pick up women. This usually includes most European-style restaurants and hotel dining rooms. Room service, of course, is an alternative. And so is safety in numbers: invite a few of the women in the office where you are doing business to join you (on *your* expense account, naturally).

2. Unless it comes from your company, do not give male colleagues any but the most perfunctory gift unless obviously earmarked for the home or children.

3. If you are (or were) married, use a Mrs. even if you don't at home.

4. Make it a point to mention your husband and children (if you have any), and also ask about your male counterpart's family. If the question of dinner arises, invite them, too.

5. As soon as you are introduced to the family, stop talking business and strike up a rapport with the others.

6. In Latin countries men make overt approaches whether they know you or not. Just returning a look on the street can give you problems. With business acquaintances a firm if unflattering no is often more diplomatic than playing it coy or ambiguous.

7. Above all, do not date anyone you are there to do business with. If he is irresistible, wait until he comes over here.

On Your Best Behavior

In the world of cultural behavior, the only truly safe generalization is: don't generalize.

"All Americans are loud and lacking in grace." "The English are cold and aloof." "The French are romantic but often rude." So it goes. And each generalization can be blasted and disproven.

Still, there are some general rules about each region and each nation. Each rule will have its exception, but an awareness of the rules places you in an advantageous and more comfortable position.

In the area of protocol, here is a potpourri of general advice.

In EUROPE, the general rule of thumb is to behave as if you were calling on a rich old auntie. While the New World may have loosened up dramatically in the past couple of generations, the Old one remains very buttoned up — literally and figuratively. What would be mildly bad manners at home (gum chewing, talking with hands in pockets, legs propped up on furniture, backslapping, etc.) are cardinal sins in Continental company. Suit coats stay on in offices and restaurants and on the street, even in July. Women do not wear pants to work or to dressy restaurants. First names are never used without invitation and that usually only comes after long association. Those with academic titles and degrees expect you to use them as a sign of respect. Except in Southern and Eastern Europe, the handshake serves as standard greeting but is executed with a much limper squeeze and with no American-style arm pumping and shoulder thwacking. For all business introductions and most personal ones, an exchange of business cards is de rigueur. Smoking at the table is frowned on until cognac and coffee are served. Punctuality is a must.

In France, they are appalled by the way anyone else speaks French — including some other Frenchmen. Unless you are urged to trot out your Berlitz lessons, it is safer to stick to English except for greetings, toasts, and an occasional isolated phrase. Be prepared to field argument, criticism, and controversial subjects such as California wine vs. French, why soccer is superior to football, etc. The French are proud of their education (much more rigorous than most Americans') and their opinions — and relish showing off both in feisty debate. They get right down to business matters but are slow to come to decisions, displaying a seemingly endless fascination with minute details. Whether the decision is good news or bad, they state their intentions unambiguously. Haute cuisine, of course, is no laughing matter, and you must pay proper respect to what is on your plate at even the most perfunctory business lunch. Many French people are offended by dinner guests who begin a meal with palate-numbing drinks like martinis and Scotch.

In Germany, gentlemen walk and sit to the left of all ladies and men of senior business rank. Men rise when a woman leaves or returns to the table. Your dinner guest will expect you to have made arrangements in advance and not show up asking, "Got any ideas where we should eat?" Formality and punctiliousness are more pronounced here than anywhere else in Europe, possibly the world.

In Great Britain, it isn't so much what you do as how you do it. The British public school (what we call private or prep school) specializes in manners and self-discipline. In business, emotions are rarely vented and protocol is given the utmost attention. In socializing, be sure to issue your invitations well in advance. The British keep engagement calendars as religiously as Boswell kept his diaries, and get-togethers are booked days — even weeks — in advance. If you get an invitation reading "black tie" or "smoking," it means men must wear dinner jackets with all the proper accompaniments from studs to black silk hose and women must wear long dresses. Renting formal wear is blessedly simple in London. Moss Bros. (pronounced as one word: "mossbros") is famous for renting (the British call it hiring) all forms of formal wear. At formal dinners the host sometimes says grace. This is a signal that after the main course the Loyal Toast will probably be offered. This is a toast to Her Majesty's health, and after that you may smoke — *but never before.* By and large, dinner at 7:30 means at 7:30. You may be ten minutes late but not ten minutes early. It is not customary to take gifts unless there is a special reason: a birthday, anniversary, or reciprocation for a gift received. The usual practice is to take flowers. If the value of the gift exceeds fifteen dollars or so, it may cause embarrassment.

Quiz: Know the difference between England, Britain, and the United Kingdom? (Most visitors don't.) England, Scotland, and Wales comprise Great Britain and when Northern Ireland is added, it becomes the United Kingdom.

Not only is British dress conservative but so is the conversation. Unlike the French, Britons prefer less controversial chitchat than politics and religion usually provide. The safest subject, particularly in England, is animals, for whether they shoot them or let them sleep in the parlor, the Queen's loyal subjects are unashamed lovers of fur, feather, and fin. It is noteworthy that in England there is a *National* Society for the Prevention of Cruelty to Children but a *Royal* Society for the Prevention of Cruelty to Animals.

Most honorary (as opposed to hereditary) titles such as sir, dame, and lord are used even among familiar acquaintances. Before addressing such a person by name, it is wise to hear how others do it.

In pubs the change you leave on the counter for your next drink may be taken as a tip by the bartender, so keep it in your pocket until you are ready to reorder. If you want bourbon, ask for it that way, because "whiskey" means Scotch. When pulling out a cigarette, always offer them to your "mates." Reason: cigarettes are, and always have been, very expensive in England. But it is also just a polite custom.

Avoid striped ties in case they are copies of British regimentals, for one does not wear an old school tie when one has not attended the old school.

Keep in mind that many "English" words have a totally different meaning from their American usage. For example: *lift* (elevator), *chemist* (druggist), *vet* (a verb meaning to examine critically or appraise), and *intercourse* (a friendly dialogue).

Elsewhere in Europe, observing the national differences between countries that, to us, perhaps seem nearly indistinguishable is very important. Austrians appreciate being recognized for their own character and accomplishments (Mozart was *not* a German) and although not the case in Germany, it is always polite in Austria to greet people in public, even complete strangers. In Belgium the Flemish and the Walloons are as different as the Dutch and the French (whence they came) and should be treated with similar distinctions; the Flemish, incidentally, kiss cheeks *three* times, alternating cheeks.

In Bulgaria, a nod means no and a shake of the head means yes.

In both Denmark and Sweden, the toast can be a very formal regimen. You must never toast your host or anyone senior to you in rank or age until they toast you, nor must you touch your drink until the host has said skoal. If you are seated at your hostess's left, you should propose a toast to her during dessert; if on her right, you are expected to make a short speech of appreciation.

In Greece, there are no rules of greeting; they may shake hands, embrace, and/or kiss at the first and every meeting. Punctuality is not a must.

Iceland is the exception to the rule of not calling people by their first names. Icelanders use first names among themselves — although they often will accommodate foreigners by using last names. Making definite appointments and getting there on time are simply not done.

In Italy, handshaking is a national pastime, but seldom do Italians remember names on first introduction. All university graduates have a title and usually expect you to use it (*dottore* for liberal arts, *avvocato* for law, *ingegnere* for technical fields, and *professore* for both professors and most medical doctors).

In the Netherlands, the toast is given just before and just after the first sip. Punctuality is a must.

In Spain, the only time you must take punctuality seriously is when attending a bullfight. Most offices and shops close for siesta all the way from 1:30 to 4:30 P.M., and restaurants do not usually reopen until after 9 or get into full swing until 11.

In Switzerland, needless to say, punctuality is a way of life (and don't complain that your watch, which is almost certainly Swiss, is slow).

The MIDDLE EAST no longer generates the mystery — or misgivings — for Western travelers that it did before "Come with me to the Casbah" became "Meet you in the conference room." Arabs are proud of their new place in the world economy and enjoy hearing outsiders acknowledge it. They also relish the facility with words that their oil-financed educations at Oxford, Yale, and the rest of the world's ivied halls have bestowed. However, to outsiders those words can be swords. Arab rhetoric and bombast, born of an ethnic tradition of high passions and short fuses that historians trace back centuries to pre-Islamic days, are not reserved for global enemies alone. An Arab is as quick to explode at friend as at foe. Not only is there no stigma attached to sounding off, but it is looked on as a handy safety valve — a first line of defense, or offense — that makes the ranter feel better without having done any real harm to the rantee.

The other side of the instant frown, however, is the instant smile. Arab preoccupation with both personal and public opinion can lead to misunderstandings. As Arab author Sania Hamady writes, "The desire to please — to pave the way for favorable and happy relationships with possible good results — may induce them to say what is agreeable without regard to truth." This, added to the habit of giving their word rather than their signature to agreements, can make an outsider believe he has a yes when the answer was really no.

Handshakes are the custom outside the home, but a host may welcome you with a kiss on both cheeks and you should reciprocate. Do not ask for an alcoholic drink unless it is offered, and do not bring the hostess a gift or inquire about her (she will almost certainly be kept out of sight and out of the conversation).

It is important to arrive at both social and business affairs on time. But do not expect to *leave* them on time. An Arab's sense of the world around him is that of an extended family, and he will interrupt even the most serious discussion to deal with whoever seeks his time and counsel. He may also stop all business several times a day to pray, either at the office or at the nearest mosque. No irritation should ever be shown at these digressions; they are an unshakable rule of Islamic life, writ not in sand but in stone.

No one expects you to speak Arabic, but a few words can be endearing to a people proud of their heritage and history. *Sahtein* is the equivalent of *bon appétit. Soufra daiman* means, roughly, "May food be always available on this table." You will probably have ample cause to use both, since Arabs are famous for their hospitality — and gargantuan banquets. Skip breakfast and lunch the day you are invited. Less likely is the opportunity to say *sahha* (cheers!), given the near nonexistence of strong drink in Islam. Pork is also forbidden. Any animal that scavenges or has a cloven hoof is shunned by devout Muslims.

A shared cup of thick coffee or mint tea usually precedes any business dealings. Giving and taking are never done with the left hand. Ditto for eating. The business week runs from Saturday to Wednesday or Thursday, with Thursday and/or Friday the Muslim day of rest and worship. No work is done after noon during Ramadan, the ninth month of the Islamic lunar calendar.

In Saudi Arabia, greetings are particularly elaborate: first, you say *salaam alaykum;* second, you shake hands, accompanied by the words *kaif halak;* next, a Saudi will often extend his left hand to your right shoulder and kiss you on both cheeks. Thereafter, he is likely to take your hand in his, publicly or privately, as a show of kinship. (If you should be entertaining a Saudi over here, you will probably find that he realizes hand holding is taboo. In case he hasn't heard, however, you might want to mention it, making a slight joke of it.)

Remember, too, that in Saudi Arabia they go by lunar time: watches are set differently, days and months do not follow our Gregorian calendar, and the year is counted from 622 A.D., the year Muhammed escaped from Mecca.

In AFRICA, there is such a diversity of language, custom, and culture that few rules reach beyond national borders and practices can vary wildly within a nation, such as Nigeria, with clearly defined tribal areas.

In LATIN AMERICA, you can behave anyway you like, as long as you are simpatico — meaning that you must feel comfortable with Latin ways before Latins will feel comfortable with you. Those ways, to a newly arrived Northerner, can be very *un*comfortable at first. Women are put off by the machismo, which runs the gamut from swaggering and flirting to taking for granted that any female over fifteen is available and no doubt willing, regardless of her marital status and his attractiveness. For men it is the opposite side of the macho coin that causes problems. Emotions are much closer to the surface (some would say feminine) and are likely to boil over into tears, rapture, fury, or sentimentality with an ease at which most American men feel uneasy. Eye contact must be unflinching. Conversation must be nose-to-nose. Shoulders are squeezed. Lapels are fondled. Hugs and two-handed handshakes are common among mere acquaintances. Hospitality and generosity are carried to what many Americans consider a fault. Admire a Latin's new gold watch and he may give it to you.

Siesta and *mañana* are two words that set many Americans' teeth on edge — the former because it means that just about everything, including stores, banks, and business offices, closes for two or three hours in early afternoon, and the latter because it means that things get done when they get done and people get there when they get there. In fact, there is a positive revulsion toward being the first to arrive. To "blend with the crowd," it is customary to arrive at least a quarter of an hour late, and in busy, traffic-jammed cities like Mexico City, it is more like an hour or even two.

It is hard to know at first meeting if a Latin identifies more with his Spanish or his Indian heritage. Better to let him reveal his sentiments before waxing poetic about one or the other, lest it be taken as a slight to the preferred bloodline.

Another practice that requires advance information is haggling over prices. It varies from country to country (yes in Mexico, no in Chile) and from shop to shop.

AUSTRALIA, although it can take twenty-six hours on a jet to get there, is as close to home as many Americans ever feel away from home. A wry Englishman visiting Chicago described it as "instant Australia." Unlike most other people who shared in World War II with us, the Australians have never forgotten it and remember warmly how the Yanks helped win the day on both sides of the world. It may be the only place on earth where American servicemen do not immediately jump into civilian clothes when off duty.

There is nothing an Australian likes better than to chat it up with a stranger at a pub. Most visitors report that it is impossible to have a lonely, morose drink by themselves, unless, of course, they are female. The surprise on this friendly, classless continent is that liberation has not reached the "second" sex yet. Here, macho does not mean ogling and innuendo. It simply designates a mateyness among men on which no woman dare intrude.

One commodity of which there is none is British reticence. One handshake or beer and you are on a first name basis. When it comes to punctuality, probably none but the Germans take it more seriously, but otherwise the Aussies are as unbuttoned and easygoing as any good ol' boy at a catfish fry.

In the FAR EAST, countries that are side by side are often as different as Nome and Honolulu. Indeed, no other continent has a greater variety of languages, races, and religions, and these often shape a nation's character more profoundly than any national border. Once you have crossed the Pacific, stop generalizing — except in one particular. Politeness. It is the one transcending trait shared by all Asians. Diffidence between individuals and harmony among the group take precedence over any personal feelings or ambitions that may be kicking and screaming inside your head.

In Japan, they never say no in public, which is why American businessmen often take away the wrong impression. But this obsession with pleasing does not mean that the Japanese make quick friends, particularly with Western businesspeople. A rollicking night out on the town will not necessarily lead to signing the contract to your advantage the next morning. *Naniwabushi* (to get on such close personal terms with someone that he will have to do you a favor) is standard Japanese operating procedure. Hence, accepting lavish gifts from a Japanese business acquaintance can lead to obligations that may later prove awkward, if not downright painful.

The People's Republic of China is the latest incarnation of the world's oldest civilization, one whose social and cultural achievements were, for centuries, the most sophisticated on earth. While visitors cannot help arriving with their own political and cultural baggage, it is polite to remember that the Chinese, too, have a very strong sense of self — of their own value system and their own style. Once known as "the giant with the tiny appetite," China more and more seeks the same economic goals as the rest of the world — but often with methods true to its most ancient traditions. The age-old obsession with keeping face is still alive and well there.

You see it in their concern with who goes through the door or sits down first. (Always let *them* have the right-of-way.)

You see it in their sensitivity to status and title. (Never rely on "Mr." to take the place of a person's proper title, such as "Committee Member" Wang, "General" Li, "Factory Manager" Hsieh, or "Bureau Chief" Chang. Also, never call anyone "Comrade" unless you are one yourself.)

And, most often, you see it in their painfully cautious deliberations in business matters. (As one Western sales representative says, "The same transaction that would take a week in New York, two in Paris, and three in Rio may take months in Beijing. And then a year after they've said yes or no, they can change their minds.")

The Chinese are superb hosts, masters of the twelve-course banquet and frequent dinner toasts. No drink but beer should be touched until a toast is proposed. This is sometimes done with a long, elaborate speech or sometimes by merely raising the glass and making eye contact. Only a symbolic sip need be taken in reply.

Chinese frequently show regard for a member of their own sex by publicly holding hands or by some other physical contact, but the opposite sexes rarely make any public show of affection. Great respect is shown to older people, and punctuality is a given.

Elsewhere in the Far East, where the Chinese culture has been exported by centuries of Chinese expatriates, expect to find much the same preoccupation with maintaining one's self-esteem. Putting a good face on even the worst situation remains a way of life even in Hong Kong and Singapore, where the English have introduced an equal dose of Westernization. Visitors are often pleasantly surprised by the serendipity of East meeting West. For example, both New Years are commonly celebrated. And while politeness and mutual respect are never given short shrift, business deals are handled with a crisp efficiency Lord Keynes might have applauded.

Just because the Chinese dominate a culture, however, it does not mean that other influences will not be encountered. In Malaysia, for instance, you will be given chopsticks and a spoon when dining with a Chinese, but if your host is a Hindu or Malay, you may get nothing at all (your hands are your utensils for the evening). Pork, of course, is a staple of Chinese cooking, but Malays will not touch it. On the other hand, Hindus and Buddhists avoid beef. Buddhists are also extremely sensitive about being touched on the head, especially in Thailand.

While the handshake takes precedence over any other greeting in most Oriental countries (except Japan), Thais still prefer the *wai* (pronounced why), which is executed by placing both hands together in a praying position at the chest. The higher the hands, the more respect you show, although eye level is the highest anyone goes. Do not ever make light of either Buddha or the royal family to a Thai, for God and King are taken with ultraseriousness. There is never any touching between the sexes (even married couples) in public, and that includes dancing. So if you hear a waltz, stay seated. Don't be surprised to be called by your first name at first meeting, as in "Mr. Bob" or "Miss Jennifer". Thais use first names in even the most formal circumstances. When shopping in Thailand, remember that except in department stores and bookstores, prices are merely an invitation to bargain and may be anywhere from 100 to 300 percent higher than the seller is willing to accept after vigorous haggling.

In India, East and West meet again in a simmering stew of contrary customs. The host who says "How do you do?" in impeccable Oxford English may nonetheless greet you with a reverential *namaste* (palms together and a nod of the head). Muslim women are kept from the view of men outside their families, and even non-Muslim women seldom show up at social functions or sit at the dinner table or join in the conversation even in their own homes. (That red dot on forehead or hair usually means a woman is married.) You will find most Indians equally well informed on love potions, magic charms, and soothsaying as they are on the international scene.

In Russia, there is no Oriental-style masking of emotions and keeping your cool. Expansiveness, generosity, and letting go are everything. Stingy is one of the worst epithets you can hurl at a Russian. All things Western, from jeans to rock 'n' roll, are idolized here. Since democratization and the move to a market economy, you may take gifts for your Russian business acquaintances. But it is still a crime for tourists to take out art objects, including religious artifacts, or to change money unofficially. The one rule you are free to break is no tipping — if you are subtle about it. Plan your trip well in advance: it takes weeks, sometimes months, to arrange visas, guides, transportation within the country, and any contacts you may need.

The gladdening of *glasnost*

Finally, before we leave the subject of rules and generalizations, a few words are in order about glasnost, the "new openness" that is sweeping the Russian steppes.

One national symbol of Russia is the *matreshka*, a series of wooden dolls, one inside another, that come in brightly painted forms and all sizes. Thanks to *glasnost*, the Western world is seeing an entirely new doll, which was kept hidden deep within the others. And because of *glasnost*, this new doll is unafraid to speak frankly and question openly.

That's good news for business travelers and curious tourists alike. Now, more than ever, Westerners can lift the curtain of sullenness, secrecy, and suspicion that insulated us from the Russian people and resulted in the historic forty-year cold war. So now is a good time to get to know them.

With or without *glasnost*, a "quick study" of the Russian people is impossible. It's like Woody Allen's claim that he once took a speed-reading course and then read *War and Peace* in eight minutes. "Want to know what it's about?" Allen confidently asked. "It's about Russia." Even reading *War and Peace* will not prepare the visitor for the vastness and diversity of the country. But we can hopscotch here and there and gain a few helpful impressions and insights. So let's start hopping:

Questions most often asked of Americans: "What are you really like? What do you care about most deeply? What is life like in America? What do other Americans think of Russians?"

Language is not an impenetrable barrier. English is taught in Russian schools beginning in third or fourth grade, so most citizens under the age of forty speak at least some English. Incidentally, to bare an American embarrassment, Russia has more teachers of English than the U.S.A. has students of Russian. So take along a phrase book to at least show you are trying.

Scenes typical of Russia today: a secondhand appearance to almost everything, churches galore, antique trolleybuses, diverse subcultures, a cornucopia of different breads, circuses everywhere, stoic faces in public but a new open curiosity and warmth in private.

Gifts to take along: printed T-shirts, quality ballpoint pens, blue jeans, rock record albums, picture books of America, chewing gum, cigarettes, country and western tapes, logoed baseball/golf caps. But take care — don't be tempted to trade in black-market goods or currency, even though trade may seem to flourish openly and it may be very tempting.

Food and drink will bring memorable experiences. Although caviar is almost as scarce (and expensive) as it is in the U.S., vodka is not. Even as vodka becomes more costly, it washes the country and lubricates the society. And prepare a repertoire of toasts; you'll make them often. The shortest and simplest one is *Nah-zda-ROE-vee-ah.* Any festive Russian meal will begin with sweet champagne and plates of *zukuski,* an appetizer of fish, meat, and pickles. Restaurant service is often glacierlike in movement, and long lines may be common at restaurants. Once inside, however, friendly Russians are known to guide Americans to the head of the line, kiss photos of your children, and try to ask questions about the U.S. in pidgin English.

Popular in Russia nowadays are: new late-night TV talk shows featuring formerly taboo topics, rock music groups complete with leotard pants, heavy metal, and studded vests, and brand name running shoes — and don't be surprised to see that hallmark of every American sidewalk and driveway, the skateboard.

Trivia and hints helpful to know: visas can be obtained through the Russian Federation (the former Soviet Embassy), Washington, D.C., or through visa agencies in major cities throughout the

U.S.; pick your destinations carefully in advance because they'll be stamped on your visa and difficult to change; public scales are a common sight throughout the country; taxis and private cars are more plentiful than before the Soviet breakup, and taxi rates are negotiable; birthdays are not celebrated as we observe them, in fact they are almost ignored; the metro (subway system) is a national prize, clean and efficient; dogs are forbidden in the cities. There are some 120 different ethnic groups in Russia.

In summary, *glasnost* has brought good tidings to the West. For the first time in many decades, the Russian people can satisfy their longing to relate to visitors. One smiling Russian writer capsuled it this way: "You lie about our country and we lie about yours. Eh? So it is. At least now we are talking openly about it . . . and smiling with each other." Chalk up one forward step for world peace and understanding.

CHAPTER 2

Hand Gestures
and
Body Language

A Risky Language
or
Actions speak louder than words—
and often say all the wrong things

"I knew I'd committed a monumental goof. But I just couldn't imagine how."

A young computer salesman from New Jersey is remembering his first overseas sales pitch. The scene was his company's offices in Rio, and it had gone like a Sunday preacher's favorite sermon. As he looked around the table, he knew he had clinched the sale. Triumphantly, he raised his hand to his Latin customers and flashed the classic American okay sign — thumb and forefinger forming a circle, other fingers pointing up.

The sunny Brazilian atmosphere suddenly felt like a deep freeze. Stony silence. Icy stares. Plus embarrassed smirks from his colleagues.

Calling for a break, they took him outside the conference room and explained. Our hero had just treated everyone to a gesture with roughly the same meaning over there as the notorious third-finger sign conveys so vividly here. Apologies saved the sale, but he still turns as pink as a Brazilian sunset when retelling the tale.

It is only natural when you find yourself at sea in the local language to use gestures to bail yourself out. Anyway, even when you can be understood, isn't it friendlier and more endearing to say it with a hand, an eye, or some other intentional body language? Yes. But only if you know what the sign is really saying. Gestures pack the power to punctuate, to dramatize, to speak a more colorful language than mere words. Yet, like the computer salesman, you may discover that those innocent winks and well-meaning nods are anything but universal.

Ever since World War II, *V* has meant "victory" all over the world. Even Winston Churchill, however, was very careful how he used it. For in Britain, unless your palm is facing outward—toward your audience—the *V* sign is the equivalent of the third finger.

> ## How Men Around the World React to Seeing a Pretty Girl
>
> - The American lifts his eyebrows.
> - The Italian presses his forefinger into his cheek and whistles.
> - The Greek strokes his cheek.
> - The Brazilian puts an imaginary telescope to his eye.
> - The Frenchman kisses his fingertips.
> - The Arab grasps his beard.

Be prepared for incoming messages, too

On his maiden trip to the Middle East, a Midwestern public relations man stepped from the cool of an ultramodern conference center into the dust and glare of an ancient roadway. Donkey carts rustled up whirlwinds of stinging sand. The air rang with a mullah's bullhorned call to prayer. Without a word, a Saudi who had attended the same conference reached down and gently took his hand. The word exotic was taking on new meaning, and the meaning set off a panic button in the visitor's brain. "What does this Arab think . . . ?" "What will all the *other* Arabs think . . . ?" Etc., etc. Finally, common sense set in. Of course, the gesture was just a simple signal of trust: silent Arabic for friendship and respect.

Even unconscious gestures can be unsettling to the uninitiated. Just back from a tour of several Arabian Gulf countries, a woman recalls how jumpy she felt talking to men there. "Not because of what they said," she explains, "but what they did with their eyes." Instead of the occasional blink, Arabs lower their lids so slowly and languorously that she was convinced they were falling asleep.

In Japan eye contact is a key to the way you feel about someone. And the less of it, the better. What a Westerner considers an honest look in the eye, the Oriental takes as a lack of respect and a personal affront. Even when shaking hands or bowing — and especially when conversing — only an occasional glance into the other person's face is considered polite. The rest of the time great attention should be paid to fingertips, desk tops, and the warp and woof of the carpet.

"Always keep your shoes shined in Tokyo," advises an electronics representative who has logged many hours there. "You can bet a lot of Japanese you meet will have their eyes on them."

On the other hand (or foot), Arabs and many Asians flinch at the sight of shoe soles. Hence, feet are best kept flat on the floor — never propped up on a table or desk or crossed over the knee.

Bye-bye no-no

In Europe the correct form for waving hello and good-bye is palm out, hand and arm stationary, fingers wagging up and down. The common American wave with the whole hand in motion means no — except in Greece, where it is an insult that is likely to get you into big trouble. In many countries hitchhiking with a thumb stuck out is also a very rude gesture. However, it is easy for a traveler to lapse into old habits, in which case — as long as you are recognized as an American — the reaction will probably be nothing worse than a frown.

Please touch (sometimes)

Touching can be a very touchy business. In most Latin lands from Venezuela to Sicily, the abrazo (hug) is as commonplace as the handshake. Between men and men — and women and women. This is also true in Slavic countries, where it is better described as a bear hug. The French sometimes add a man-to-man peck on the cheek.

The Japanese, though, have an aversion to casual body contact. While most Japanese who come to the West make the concession of shaking hands, they remain more comfortable at home with the traditional bow from the waist. The proper form is with hands sliding down toward the knees or at the sides, back and neck stiff, and eyes averted.

Their democratic sensibilities quivering like whiskers on a catfish, many Americans regard bowing as out-and-out kowtowing. In Japan, where there is nothing demeaning or obsequious about it, the bow remains the time-honored way of saying, "I respect your experience and wisdom." When in doubt do it anyway. It works.

For the casual encounter one brief all-purpose bow will fill the bill. But on formal occasions — a high-level business meeting, say — the true Oriental bow with all its delicate gradations may turn out to be the only medium you and your opposite number have with which to communicate. A Wall Street investment banker and veteran of countless American-Japanese conferences explains why.

"For us Westerners," he points out, "it's risky to try enunciating anything more complicated than 'sayonara.' As for the Japanese executive, the more senior he is, the less likely he is to understand English — he has an army of ambitious underlings to understand it for him. His seniority also means he has not come to the meeting to do business — those decisions have already been made at a lower level."

So why is he there at all? "Mainly, to see who it is he's doing business *with*." Hence, on these occasions form is frequently more telling than content.

With business inferiors: Always allow them to bow lower and longer than you do.

With equals: Match bows, adding an extra one when you want to show a slight edge of respect, as with someone substantially older than you or with a customer whose business you are trying to get.

When unsure of status: The safest move is to bow a shade less low than the other person.

With the top man: If he clearly outranks you, make sure you outbow him even if it takes your knuckles all the way to the floor. Also, remember to keep your eyes respectfully lowered. Which, of course, isn't easy when you are trying to see how low *he* is bowing to *you*.

And, in Japan never bow with a hand — or both hands — in your pockets. In fact, never shake hands or give a speech with hand-in-pocket.

Learn all this and you'll become a Laurence Olivier in the art of bowing.

International Gesture Dictionary

Gestures Using the Face

Eyebrow Raise: In Tonga, a gesture meaning "yes" or "I agree." In Peru, means "money" or "Pay me."

Blink: In Taiwan, blinking the eyes at someone is considered impolite.

Wink: Winking at women, even to express friendship, is considered improper in Australia.

Eyelid Pull: In Europe and some Latin American countries, means "Be alert" or "I am alert."

Ear Flick: In Italy, signifies that a nearby gentleman is effeminate.

Ear Grasp: Grasping one's ears is a sign of repentance or sincerity in India. A similar gesture in Brazil — holding the lobe of one's ear between thumb and forefinger — signifies appreciation.

Nose Circle: The classic American "okay" sign — the fingers circle — is placed over the nose in Colombia to signify that the person in question is homosexual.

Nose Tap: In Britain, secrecy or confidentiality. In Italy, a friendly warning.

Nose Thumb: One of Europe's most widely known gestures, signifying mockery. May be done double-handed for greater effect.

Nose Wiggle: In Puerto Rico, "What's going on?"

Cheek Screw: Primarily an Italian gesture of praise.

Cheek Stroke: In Greece, Italy, and Spain, means "attractive." In Yugoslavia, "success." Elsewhere, it can mean "ill" or "thin."

Fingertips Kiss: Common throughout Europe, particularly in Latin countries (and in Latin America). Connotes "aah, beautiful!," the object of which may be anything from a woman or a wine to a Ferrari or a soccer play. Origin probably dates to the custom of ancient Greeks and Romans who, when entering and leaving the temple, threw a kiss toward sacred objects such as statues and altars.

Head Screw: In Germany, a strong symbol meaning "You're crazy." Often used by drivers on the autobahn to comment on the driving skills of other travelers, this gesture can get you arrested! The same gesture is used in Argentina, but without the consequences.

Chin Flick: "Not interested," "Buzz off," in Italy. In Brazil and Paraguay, "I don't know."

Head Circle: In most European and some Latin American countries, a circular motion of the finger around the ear means "crazy." In the Netherlands, it means someone has a telephone call.

Head Nod: In Bulgaria and Greece, signifies "no." In most other countries, "yes."

Head Tap: In Argentina and Peru, "I'm thinking" or "Think." Elsewhere it can mean "He's crazy."

Head Tilt: In Paraguay, tilting the head backwards means "I forgot."

Head Toss: In southern Italy, Malta, Greece, and Tunisia, a negation. In Germany and Scandinavia, a beckoning motion. In India, "yes."

Hand and Arm Gestures

Horizontal Horns: A gesture of self-protection against evil spirits in most European countries. In some African countries, a variation — pointing the index and third finger toward someone — can be interpreted as putting the "evil eye" on him. Use with discretion.

Vertical Horns: In Italy, signifies that you are being cuckolded. But in Brazil and other parts of Latin America, can be a sign of good luck.

V **Sign:** In most of Europe, means "victory" when, as Churchill did, you keep your palm facing away from you. The same gesture palm *in* means, roughly, "Shove it." In non-British-oriented countries, it generally means two of something, as in "Two more beers, please." It was, by the way, not an Englishman but a Belgian who first made the *V* synonymous with victory in World War II.

Beckon: To use finger(s) to call someone is insulting to most Middle and Far Easterners. It is proper in most of these countries, and in Portugal, Spain, and Latin America, to beckon someone with palm down, fingers or whole hand waving.

Fingers Circle: Widely accepted as the American "okay" sign, except in Brazil and Germany, where it's considered vulgar or obscene. The gesture is also considered impolite in Greece and Russia, while in Japan, it signifies "money," and in southern France, "zero" or "worthless."

Fingers Cross: In Europe, crossed fingers have several meanings, most commonly "protection" or "good luck." In Paraguay, the gesture may be offensive.

Fingers Snap: In France and Belgium, snapping the fingers of both hands has a vulgar meaning. In Brazil, it connotes something done long ago or for a long time.

47

One-Finger Point: In most Middle and Far Eastern countries, pointing with the index finger is considered impolite. The open hand is used instead, or, in Indonesia, the thumb.

Two-Finger Tap: In Egypt, this means a couple is sleeping together and, true or false, is always rude. Can also mean, "Would you like to sleep together?"

Third-Finger Thrust: Not nice in any language, this old favorite has survived for more than 2,000 years. (The Romans called the third finger the "impudent" finger.)

Third-Finger Reverse: Same meaning as executed by an Arab.

Fist slap: " _____ you" in Italy, Chile, and many other places.

Forearm Jerk: Another way of saying the above or some variation thereof, especially in

Mediterranean countries.

In England, however, it connotes a sexual compliment, equivalent to a wolf whistle.

Thumbs Up: In Australia, a rude gesture; in almost every other place in the world, simply means "okay."

Flat-Hand Flick: The universal flicking of the fingers toward the source of irritation, meaning "Go away" or "Get lost."

Palm Push: In Nigeria, pushing the palm of the hand forward with fingers spread is a vulgar gesture.

Hand Pat: In Holland, "He/she is gay."

Hand Purse: Can signify a question or good or fear. Considered almost the national gesture of Italy.

Hand Saw: When you make a deal in Colombia and intend to share the profits, the gesture is: one palm facing down with the other hand making a sawing motion across the back of the hand facing down.

Hand Sweep: In Latin America and the Netherlands, a sweeping or grabbing motion made toward your body, as though you were sweeping chips off a table, means that someone is stealing or "getting away with something." The same gesture in Peru means "money" or "Pay me."

Waving: Called the *moutza* in Greece, this is a serious insult, and the closer the hand to the other person's face, the more threatening it is considered. Same in Nigeria. Never use it to get a waiter's or cabdriver's attention. In Europe, raise the palm outward and wag the fingers in unison to wave "good-bye." Waving the whole hand back and forth can signify "no," while in Peru, that gesture means, "Come here."

Height: In Colombia and much of Latin America, only an animal's height is indicated by using the whole hand, palm down. It is polite to hold the palm facing the observer to

show human height, or, in Mexico, to use the index finger.

The *Wai*: Traditional greeting in Thailand. Called the *namaste* in India.

Arms Fold: In Finland, folded arms are a sign of arrogance and pride. In Fiji, the gesture shows disrespect.

Elbow Tap: In Holland, "He's unreliable." In Colombia, "You are stingy."

The Fig: In some European and Mediterranean countries, an obscene gesture of contempt. In Brazil and Venezuela, a symbol of

good luck reproduced in such diverse forms as paperweights and golden amulets worn around the neck.

SPECIAL SECTION

A Quick Guide
to the
Ways of the World

This section has been compiled in an effort to provide the fast-moving international business executive — as well as the casual tourist — with a quick, helpful reference list. Countries are grouped by regions of the world and are arranged alphabetically within groups. For more details on a specific country, refer to the Index.

Europe

With the dizzying pace of change throughout Europe, almost everyone is aware that many old names no longer apply. East and West Germany have become simply Germany. Czechoslovakia is now split into two separate republics: the Czech Republic and the Slovak Republic. And at this writing, what will happen in Yugoslavia is anyone's guess.

As for the former Soviet Union, at this writing the shake-up shapes up as follows: Of the fifteen former Soviet republics, eleven are now members of the Commonwealth of Independent States (CIS), a loose union of independent nations that has succeeded the U.S.S.R. in some aspects of international affairs. The CIS member states are Armenia, Azerbaijan, Belorussia, Moldavia, Russia, and Ukraine, plus the central Asian republics of Kazakhstan, Kirghizia, Tajikistan, Turkmenistan, and Uzbekistan. The three Baltic republics — Estonia, Latvia, and Lithuania — are recognized as independent states, as is Georgia.

Once they have figured out *where* they are headed, travelers to the relabeled Europe will want to remember these general tips.

General Protocol
What would be mildly bad manners at home (gum chewing, talking with hands in pockets, legs propped up on furniture, backslapping, etc.) are cardinal sins in Continental company.

Names/Greetings
First names are never used without invitation and that usually comes only after long association. Those with academic titles and degrees expect you to use them as a sign of respect.

Except in Southern and Eastern Europe, the handshake serves as standard greeting but is executed with a much limper squeeze and with no American-style arm pumping and shoulder thwacking.

For all business introductions and most personal ones, an exchange of business cards is *de rigueur*.

Appointments/Punctuality
Punctuality is a must, especially in Northern European countries.

Hospitality/Gift Giving
Smoking at the table is usually frowned on until cognac and coffee are served.

Sending flowers is a safe and appreciated gift gesture.

Dress
Suit coats stay on in offices, in restaurants, and on the street.

Women do not wear pants to work or to dressy restaurants.

Austria

General Protocol
Austrians appreciate being recognized for their own character and accomplishments. Never call an Austrian a German. While they speak the same language, Austrians and Germans have distinct customs and different values.

Although not the case in Germany, it is always polite here to greet people in public, even complete strangers.

Appointments/Punctuality
Arrange business appointments in advance and try to be punctual.

Hospitality/Gift Giving
Give flowers or some small gift such as chocolates when invited to a home for the first time for dinner or for a visit other than business. But avoid red roses (connoting romantic affection), red carnations (reserved for May Day), and an even number of flowers (considered bad luck).

Conversation
Avoid discussions about money, religion, or politics unless you are specifically asked about them.

Belgium

General Protocol
Privacy is a jealously guarded right and is carefully respected.

Names/Greetings
In Belgium cheek kissing is done three times, alternating cheeks. Do not be surprised to see men embracing.

It is customary to shake hands to greet and say good-bye to each person at a social or business gathering.

Appointments/Punctuality
Punctuality is very important.

Hospitality/Gift Giving
Avoid sending a gift of chrysanthemums. They are a reminder of death.

Conversation
Politics, local language differences (French-Flemish), and religion are generally topics to be avoided. The Belgians will often tell jokes about the Dutch — and vice versa. Better to stay out of that regional rivalry.

Bulgaria

Names/Greeting
A handshake is the usual form of greeting.

Appointments/Punctuality
Make business appointments far in advance. Be punctual.

Hospitality/Gift Giving
If you are invited to a home, take flowers, candy, or wine.

Conversation
Avoid discussing politics and social conditions in Bulgaria.

Gestures
A nod means 'no' and a shake of the head from side to side means 'yes.'

The Czech Republic
(See The Slovak Republic page 68.)

General Protocol
Avoid taking photographs in museums or art galleries. Do not photograph military installations.

Names/Greetings
When greeting a person with a professional title, such as doctor or professor, always use the title before the surname.

Men shake hands when meeting. A man should wait for a woman to offer her hand first.

Appointments/Punctuality
Make business appointments far in advance. Be punctual.

Hospitality/Gift Giving
If you are invited to a home, take flowers (an odd number), except red roses, which have romantic implications, wine, whiskey, or cognac.

Conversation
Avoid being drawn into emotional or personal discussions of politics, religion, and social conditions. A safe topic of conversation: sports.

Denmark

General Protocol
No taxi tipping — also no tipping on restaurant and hotel bills.

Names/Greetings
Shake hands — both men's and women's.

Appointments/Punctuality
Like all Scandinavians, Danes love the summer months. It's difficult — and inconsiderate — to conduct heavy business in July and August.

Punctuality is a must.

Hospitality/Gift Giving
Toasting with a skoal is common — directly to an individual or to the whole crowd.

If you are the guest of honor, you will be seated to the left of the hostess. It is a Danish custom for the guest of honor to raise a glass after the meal and thank the hostess (in suitably flowery language) for the excellent cuisine.

Danes like to surprise others with their potent aquavit (literally, "water of life"). So be forewarned.

It is impolite to leave your host's home too soon after dinner.

A bouquet of flowers taken to the home will always be well received.

Men might consider packing a tuxedo because senior businessmen stage more black-tie dinners than in other countries.

England, Scotland, and Wales

General Protocol
In business, emotions are rarely vented and protocol is given the utmost attention. However, you may find the Welsh and Scots more informal than the British.

Avoid the word "English." You'll please everyone if you use the word "British."

The *Scotch* is what you drink. The people are called *Scots* or *Scotsmen*. Tartans, terriers, and the language itself are *Scottish*.

Names/Greetings

Most honorary titles are used, even among familiar acquaintances. But it is wise to first hear how others address a person.

It is increasingly common for business associates to use first names, even on first acquaintance.

Appointments/Punctuality

Appointments are essential. You may be ten minutes late but not ten minutes early.

Hospitality/Gift Giving

As soon as the day is done, so is business, and nothing turns your hosts off faster than continuing shoptalk over drinks and dinner.

Invitations to people's homes are much more forthcoming than in most Northern European countries. Be sure to issue *your* invitations well in advance.

An invitation reading "black tie" or "smoking" means men must wear dinner jackets with all the proper accompaniments from studs to black silk hose and women must wear long dresses.

Businessmen are not usually invited home for dinner, as most business entertaining is done in pubs and restaurants. However, should you be invited to dinner at a British home, flowers and chocolates would be a suitable gift to the lady of the house on arrival. Avoid white lilies. They suggest death.

You may smoke after the toast to Her Majesty's health but *never* before.

Entertainment in the form of lunch, dinner, drinks, or a night at the theater or ballet usually takes the place of gift giving.

Dinner is coming to replace the noon meal as the main meal of the day, although the institution of the business lunch is still going strong.

Dress

Avoid striped ties in case they are copies of British regimentals.

Conversation

What not to talk about: politics, gossip about the monarchy, and religion. Avoid starting a conversation with "What do you do?" That's considered rather personal.

Gestures

Ever since World War II, the *V* sign has meant "victory" all over the world. But be sure your palm is facing outward — toward your audience.

In Wales avoid beckoning to someone with your arms.

Finland

General Protocol
There are differences, of course, among the five Nordic countries, but for the visitor from abroad, the similarities may be more important than the differences. Although Finland is linguistically and racially different from its neighbors, the customs and life-style of the Scandinavian people are rather homogenous.

Service charges are generally added to restaurant and hotel bills, so tipping is rare. No taxi tipping.

Names/Greetings
Finns greet each other with a firm handshake. Hugs and kisses are saved for close friends and family.

Appointments/Punctuality
Avoid scheduling business trips to Finland in June and July.

Appointments should be made well in advance. Be punctual.

Hospitality/Gift Giving
If you are invited to a Finnish home for dinner, take some flowers for the hostess.

Alcohol is often consumed in great quantities and varieties at dinners, so be wary if unaccustomed to heavy drinking. Also be aware that in Finland, as in all Nordic countries, drunk driving laws are strict and should be strictly obeyed.

Although Finns are not formal people, a toast generally is drunk at the beginning of a meal. In addition to dinner, guests may be invited to take a sauna with the host, but mixed gender saunas are not common.

Conversation
Good topics of conversation include hobbies, sports, and travel. Finns also enjoy discussing politics — but keep it in mind that Finland is a multiparty system with a multitude of political views.

France

General Protocol
French businessmen tend to be rather formal and conservative.

Natives are appalled by the way anyone else speaks French — including some other Frenchmen.

In Western Europe, logo gifts should be
in good taste and unobtrusive.

Names/Greetings
A light handshake is the usual form of greeting, but a visitor should not offer his hand to a person of superior authority.

Appointments/Punctuality
Prior appointments are the rule. Punctuality is a sign of courtesy.

Hospitality/Gift Giving
An invitation to visit someone's home, even after long acquaintance, is rare. But for that occasion, a small gift of flowers (not roses or chrysanthemums) or chocolates for the hostess will be appreciated.

Cuisine, and therefore noon and evening meals, are an important and respected part of daily life.

Gifts that appeal to intellect or esthetics are especially appreciated. Avoid gifts with large, prominent stamps of your company name.

Conversation
Avoid personal questions, politics, and money as topics of conversation.

Germany

General Protocol
Although Germany is now one unified country, there are still remnants of sensitivities from the post-World War II days, when the country was divided into East and West.

Names/Greetings
Handshakes all around are customary on meeting and leaving.

Respect titles (*Doktor*) and *never* jump to a first name basis until invited.

Conversation among strangers usually employs the formal *Sie*, with a capital *S* if written. The use of the more intimate *du* together with the first name must be mutually agreed upon, except among young people or in progressive circles, where the general use of *du* indicates a less formal style.

Appointments/Punctuality
Appointments must be made and punctuality is essential. Make appointments well in advance. Should you be unable to keep an appointment, cancel or postpone it by phone.

Hospitality/Gift Giving
Invitations to German homes are a special privilege. A man should bring flowers, which he will unwrap in the entrance hall and present to the hostess upon greeting her. Avoid red roses, as

they have romantic implications, and never give thirteen or an even number of flowers.

A thank-you note should be sent within a few days for any hospitality.

Conversation
Avoid references to baseball, basketball, or American football. Instead, talk about the German countryside, hobbies, and such sports as soccer.

Greece

General Protocol
The elderly are respected, addressed by courteous titles, served first, and have much authority.

Names/Greetings
There are no rules for greeting. Greeks may shake hands, embrace, and/or kiss at the first and every meeting.

Appointments/Punctuality
While prior appointments are not usually necessary, the courtesy of phoning ahead will be appreciated. Punctuality is not a must.

Hospitality/Gift Giving
Greek hospitality is sincere, incredibly generous, and sometimes overwhelming. Be careful not to praise a specific object or the host may insist on giving it to you.

If you are invited to a Greek home, take flowers or a cake for the hostess.

The main meal of the day is lunch, which is served between noon and 2 P.M.

Conversation
Topics to avoid in conversation: Cyprus and other controversial aspects of international politics closely affecting Greece.

Gestures
A slight upward nod of the head means "no," not "yes," and tilting the head to either side means "yes" or "of course."

A Greek sometimes may smile when very angry.

Hungary

General Protocol
Do not photograph soldiers or military installations.

Names/Greetings
The customary greeting is a handshake; a man should wait for a woman to extend her hand first.

Hospitality/Gift Giving
If you are invited to dinner at home, take Western liquor or wrapped flowers (but not red roses) as a gift.

Conversation
Good topics of conversation: food, wine, what you like about Hungary. Avoid discussing politics or religion.

Iceland

General Protocol
Service charges are included in restaurant bills, and tipping is considered an insult.

Names/Greetings
Icelanders use first names among themselves, but they expect foreigners to use their last name and will use last names when speaking to foreigners. In many cases they will soon go over to using first names.

Appointments/Punctuality
Business appointments are not usually necessary, as a tradition of "dropping in" prevails. Punctuality is not a must.

Hospitality/Gift Giving
It is common, but not compulsory, to take a small gift for the host or hostess when you are invited to a meal.

Ireland

General Protocol
It is customary for visitors using the phone to offer to pay for the call.

Appointments/Punctuality
Make business appointments in advance, but keep it in mind that the Irish are not very time conscious.

Hospitality/Gift Giving
If you are invited to an Irish home, a gift of flowers or chocolates for the hostess will be appreciated. If you are invited to dinner, good gifts also include a bottle of wine, or cheese.
Giving business gifts is not a common practice.

Conversation
Avoid discussion of religion or politics.

Israel

General Protocol
Remember, Israel is surrounded by Arab countries, and customs, in most cases, are completely different from those of its neighbors.

The Sabbath (Saturday) is strictly observed by Orthodox Jews from nightfall on Friday to nightfall on Saturday.

Names/Greetings
Shalom is the usual greeting, on both meeting and departing.

Titles are even less important in Israel than in the U.S.

Visitors should not be surprised or offended by being called by their first name.

Appointments/Punctuality
Prior appointments are necessary. Even though Israelis in general are casual about time, you should be punctual.

Hospitality/Gift Giving
An invitation to visit should be responded to by setting a time, date, and place.

A gift of a book is an excellent choice since most Israelis are eager readers. Flowers are also appreciated.

Dress
Style of dress is more casual than in most Western countries.

Conversation
Subjects to avoid in conversation: religion, and the large amount of U.S. aid that has helped the country to survive.

Italy

General Protocol
It is customary to tip room maids, porters, and parking attendants, and to leave a small tip for waiters, even if the bill includes service charges.

Names/Greetings
Handshaking and gesturing are national pastimes.

All university graduates have a title, and they usually expect you to use it.

Appointments/Punctuality
Punctuality is not an Italian virtue — at least not for social events. Make business appointments well in advance.

Hospitality/Gift Giving
Lunch is the biggest meal of the day and on special occasions may last two or three hours.

To refuse a very insistent invitation to lunch or dinner is considered ungracious. If the occasion takes place at home, you should take wine, flowers, or chocolates. Avoid taking chrysanthemums, which are only used for funerals. Take an odd number of flowers or a dozen.

The exchange of business gifts is quite common in Italy.

Conversation
Common topics for discussion include soccer, family affairs, business, and local news.

Topics to avoid in conversation: American football, and politics.

Luxembourg

General Protocol
Although the country maintains close ties with all its larger neighbors, the people highly appreciate being recognized for their own character and achievements.

Names/Greetings
In Luxembourg cheek kissing is done twice, alternating cheeks, but only between people who are well acquainted. The handshake is quite common among both men and women.

Appointments/Punctuality
Prior appointments are appreciated. Be punctual.

Hospitality/Gift Giving
If invited to a home, you may take flowers for the hostess or have them delivered by the florist (any flowers except chrysanthemums, which, as everywhere in Western Europe, are only for the cemeteries on All Souls' Day). Alternatively, take the local brand of chocolates (highly appreciated even beyond the borders of the country).

Conversation
French and German are widely understood and spoken, as is English to a slightly lesser degree. The use of even a few words of the national language (Luxembourgish) would be highly appreciated.

The Netherlands

General Protocol
Do not tip your taxi driver.

Names/Greetings
Titles are used in formal correspondence; in other situations less formality is appropriate.

It is the custom to shake hands in greeting everyone present, including children.

Appointments/Punctuality
Prior appointments are expected, as is punctuality.

Hospitality/Gift Giving
It is customary to give flowers, chocolates, or something similar as a gift. Gifts that are novel and new are appreciated. They should be gift wrapped. Do not include food as a gift.

A toast is given just before and just after the first sip.

Conversation
The Dutch people appreciate compliments on their furniture, artwork, carpeting, and other home furnishings.

Conversation topics to avoid: American politics, money, and prices.

Good topics to discuss: Dutch politics, travel, and sports.

Norway

Names/Greetings
Until they get to know you, Norwegians are more restrictive than Americans in using first names.

Appointments/Punctuality
Norwegian businesspeople are strong on punctuality and precision. Should you be unable to keep an appointment, cancel or postpone it by phone.

Avoid business trips to Norway at Eastertime (the ten days after Palm Sunday) and in July and early August.

Hospitality/Gift Giving
If invited to a Norwegian home, bring a small gift of flowers or chocolates for the hostess.

Laws in Norway are harsh about drunk driving, so in social gatherings one person may be designated the driver — and that person abstains from alcohol.

Conversation
Personal topics such as employment, salary, and social status usually are avoided.

Good topics of conversation include hobbies, politics, sports, and travel.

Poland

Names/Greetings
First names are used by close friends only.

Appointments/Punctuality
Prior appointments are absolutely necessary.

Hospitality/Gift Giving
It is customary to take flowers for the hostess (an odd number only) for even a brief visit. They should be handed to the hostess unwrapped. A word of caution: red roses may denote romantic love.

Toasting is often a part of both formal and informal dinners.

Consumption of hard liquor is widespread in Poland and you may well be plied with cognac at business and other meetings.

Conversation
Good topics of conversation include Poland and its cultural history, life in the U.S., and your family and its activities.

Portugal

General Protocol
Gratuities are often included in the check, but it is appropriate to tip an additional 10 percent.

Names/Greetings
It is the custom in Portugal for men to greet each other with the *abraço* (embrace) — an enthusiastic hugging and mutual slapping of backs. For women a kiss on both cheeks is customary between close acquaintances.

Appointments/Punctuality
Businessmen should avoid making appointments between noon and three o'clock in the afternoon, when everything closes down. Prior appointments are absolutely necessary. While the Portuguese do not stress punctuality, the visitor should be prompt.

Hospitality/Gift Giving
You are not obliged to take a gift if you are invited to dinner. Instead, return the favor by taking your hosts to a restaurant.

Conversation
A visitor should avoid discussing politics and government.

It is polite to converse about the family, positive aspects of Portugal, and personal interests, although it is impolite to be overly inquisitive.

Romania

Names/Greetings
First name greetings generally are appropriate only between close friends. In more formal settings use a person's title and surname.

Appointments/Punctuality
Prior appointments are necessary. Romanians are very punctual, so be on time.

Hospitality/Gift Giving
Romanians consider it a great honor to entertain guests, so visitors usually will be invited out often.

If invited to a Romanian home, which is rare, don't forget flowers for the hostess (but avoid red roses).

Gifts for your host's family could include perfume, cosmetics, jeans, or coffee. Gifts for a businessman could include imprinted pens or lighters — of the inexpensive variety.

Conversation
Good topics of conversation include sports, travel, music, fashion, and books.

Avoid discussing politics or any negative aspects of Romania.

Russia

General Protocol
It is a serious crime for visitors to export art objects or to change money with private citizens.

Never drop anything — not even an old cinema ticket — in the street. It's both offensive to Russian neatness and illegal.

Plan your trip to Russia well in advance. It will take weeks, even months, to arrange visas, and travel details.

Names/Greetings
A Russian will shake hands and state his or her name when meeting someone for the first time. Greetings among friends often include hugging and kisses on the cheek.

Appointments/Punctuality
Be punctual for appointments.

Hospitality/Gift Giving
It is a common practice for guests to take flowers or liquor when invited to a Russian home. A gift of artwork or a book would be appreciated.

The Slovak Republic
(See The Czech Republic page 55.)

General Protocol
Despite the split of Czechoslovakia into two separate countries —
the Czech Republic and the Slovak Republic — customs in the
two neighbors are likely to be more similar than not. These Slavic
peoples speak similar languages, and as of January 1993 they
were maintaining a common currency and customs union. But
keep in mind that the lower standard of living in the Slovak
Republic may be a source of friction.

Spain

Names/Greetings
Men who are close friends often give each other an abrazo (hug).
Women friends greet and part with a slight embrace and a kiss on
each cheek.

Appointments/Punctuality
A break — the siesta — in the middle of the day allows families to
be together for the main meal of the day. Most offices and stores
are closed between 1:30 and 4:30 P.M.

The only time punctuality is taken seriously is when
attending a bullfight.

Hospitality/Gift Giving
An oddity in Spain is the lateness at which people eat dinner.
Restaurants do not generally open until after nine and do not get
into full swing until about eleven.

You may take flowers when you are invited to dinner (avoid
dahlias and chrysanthemums, as they are associated with death).
Other gifts could include pastries, cakes, and chocolates.

Guests are sometimes presented with a gift, which should be
opened immediately.

Conversation
Good topics of conversation include politics (but it is best to avoid
political comparisons between Spain and the U.S.), sports, and
travel.

Avoid discussions of religion, family, and job. Do not make
negative remarks about bullfighting, which is considered more an
art than a sport.

Sweden

General Protocol
Knowledge of the cultural differences among Sweden, Norway, Denmark, and Finland is a sign of thoughtfulness.

Appointments/Punctuality
Punctuality is a must, especially when invited to a Swedish home.

Hospitality/Gift Giving
A bouquet of flowers for the hostess will be appreciated.

Because of severe penalties for driving while intoxicated, one person in your social gathering will be designated driver and will avoid alcohol.

Toasting can be more formal than in the other Scandinavian countries. For example, your Swedish hosts might be impressed if you were aware of these (somewhat old-fashioned) rules:

- Never toast your host or anyone senior to you in rank or age until they toast you.

- Don't touch your drink until the host has said "skoal."

- To be very, very proper, the skoal motion is: move the glass from the waistline up to the eyes, look the other person directly in the eyes, say "skoal," drink, make a wave of the glass toward your host's eyes, and bring it back down to the table.

Conversation
Discussions may range over many different topics, but criticism of Swedish culture or politics should be avoided.

Switzerland

General Protocol
The Swiss are generally a conservative people, and they consider it impolite to be showy about wealth.

Appointments/Punctuality
Appointments are essential and punctuality is highly valued.

Avoid making appointments during July and August — the vacation time.

Hospitality/Gift Giving
At dinner the best compliment guests can give is to take second helpings of the food.

Impersonal gifts such as flowers or candy are in very good taste. Red roses, however, carry a romantic connotation.

Conversation
Good topics of conversation include sports, what you like about Switzerland, travel, and politics.

Topics to avoid: weight watching and diets (especially during meals), and questions about a person's age, job, family, or personal life.

Turkey

General Protocol
Before entering a mosque, you should remove your shoes, as the Muslims do. In the countryside the people remove their shoes before entering a home, but that is no longer the custom in the cities.

Appointments/Punctuality
Make appointments well in advance and be punctual.

Hospitality/Gift Giving
Hospitality in Turkey is sincere, generous, and sometimes overwhelming.

A Turkish businessman may invite you to his home, but he is more likely to take you to a restaurant for a leisurely evening.

If you are invited home for dinner, take flowers, candy, or pastries. If you know the family serves alcoholic beverages, you could take wine.

Dress
Turks often judge people by the way they are dressed. The rule is to dress conservatively.

Conversation
Good topics for discussion: noncontroversial international affairs, family, professions, and hobbies.

Yugoslavia

As this book goes to press, the horrors of war, "ethnic cleansing," and food and medical shortages, plus an unstable political climate, cast uncertainty over the future of foreign business dealings in the former Yugoslav republics. However, many of the following rules of protocol may still apply in Bosnia and Herzegovina, Croatia, Macedonia, Slovenia, and Yugoslavia (once Serbia and Montenegro).

Appointments/Punctuality
Appointments are necessary and Yugoslavs are generally punctual.

Hospitality/Gift Giving
A guest is always offered a snack and a drink, usually tea, coffee, or some kind of liquor. It is not improper to ask for something else.

Toasting often is a part of even informal lunches and dinners.

Take flowers — an odd number but never thirteen — or wine to dinner. Chocolates, whiskey, or coffee beans are welcome gifts.

Conversation
Good topics for discussion include life-styles in the U.S., sports, family, and fashion.

Topics to avoid in conversation: religion and, particularly, sensitive political issues.

Africa

The African continent is divided into three distinct regions:

- The northern nations, bound together by language (Arabic), religion (Islam), and resources (oil). Incidentally, it is these shared elements that form the Arab grouping: there is no such thing as an "Arab" race or nationality.

- The black countries.

- South Africa.

Each of the countries of these three regions has distinct cultural characteristics, depending, of course, on its history and on the influence of the country that colonized it. As for general rules, the northern African nations follow Arab protocol, gestures, etiquette, and behavior; the middle African nations are oriented to black multicultures; and South Africa is Dutch/English-oriented.

Algeria

Names/Greetings
Handshaking is common, both on meeting and leaving. Kissing on both cheeks (as a form of greeting only) is also common among both men and women.

Visitors are always addressed by their title and last name. Professional titles are widely used.

Appointments/Punctuality
Prior appointments are recommended. Punctuality is not widely regarded.

Hospitality/Gift Giving
When visiting, it is usually considered in good taste to devote some time to small talk — inquiring about health and family, among other polite topics — before making a smooth transition to the topic of the visit. During a second visit, it is also considered appropriate by some to give a small gift as a token of friendship.

Conversation
Topics to be avoided in conversation: politics and industrial problems.

Topics suitable for discussion: the increase in industrialization and agrarian reforms.

Côte d'Ivoire (Ivory Coast)

General Protocol
Since 1985 the official name of the country has been Côte d'Ivoire.

The official language is French, but English is spoken in all major hotels, restaurants, and administrative offices.

Tipping is not compulsory, as most hotel and restaurant bills include a service charge.

Names/Greetings
Handshaking is customary.

Appointments/Punctuality
Make appointments well in advance and be punctual. You will probably be asked to wait a few minutes.

It is advisable, when introducing yourself to the secretary of your host, to present your business card.

Hospitality/Gift Giving
Gift giving is not compulsory, but a product of your country — for instance, an imprinted or engraved ballpoint pen — would be welcome.

Egypt

General Protocol
Egyptians feel it is important to establish a feeling of friendship and trust before business is transacted.

Remember to remove your shoes before entering a mosque.

Names/Greetings
Greetings are very expressive and elaborate, with the host welcoming the visitor many times.

Appointments/Punctuality
The workweek runs from Saturday to Thursday. Friday is the Muslim day of rest.

Hospitality/Gift Giving
Social engagements usually begin later than they do in the U.S. and dinner may not be served until 10:30 or later.

When invited to dine, it is customary to take a gift of flowers or chocolates. Giving and receiving gifts should be done with both hands or the right hand — never with the left.

When entertaining Egyptians, be sure to have some nonalcoholic drinks on hand, even though the consumption of alcoholic beverages is becoming more widely accepted.

It is considered impolite to eat everything on your plate.

Conversation
One subject to avoid in conversation: Middle Eastern politics.

Topics suitable for discussion: Egyptian advancement and achievement, the positive reputation of Egyptian leaders, Egyptian cotton, and their ancient civilization.

Ghana

General Protocol
Because of the wide degree of difference among the ethnic groups, it is difficult to describe any particular custom that is practiced all over the country.

Names/Greetings
It is customary to shake hands when meeting people and when leaving.

Appointments/Punctuality
Make appointments well in advance and be punctual, although Ghanaians may be late or may not show up at all.

Gestures
Avoid gesturing with your left hand.

Kenya

General Protocol
The British call it "Keen-ya," but the more proper pronunciation is "Ken-ya," after the modern-day founder, Jomo Kenyatta.

After English, Swahili is the language most common, and the word for "hello" is the delightful-sounding *jambo*.

If you have a new product to sell, you are advised to call on the chief purchasing officer of the Ministry of Works.

Ask people before taking their picture. A tip is usually expected.

Names/Greetings
It is customary to shake hands when meeting people and when leaving.

Appointments/Punctuality
Prior appointments are necessary.

Hospitality/Gift Giving
A small gift, such as cookies or candy, should be brought when visiting. Don't bring flowers except when expressing condolences.

Conversation
Subjects to avoid in conversation: local politics and the Mau Mau period of the 1950s.

Libya

General Protocol
The economy is almost wholly state-controlled.

A traveler should be aware of current regulations on health, visas, currency, and commercial and security matters.

Appointments/Punctuality
Make appointments well in advance and be punctual — even though there is little regard for keeping a schedule in Libya.

Hospitality/Gift Giving
Hospitality will generally involve invitations to meals or receptions. There are strict laws on the prohibition of alcohol.

If you are invited to a Libyan home for dinner, only men will be present. Take a gift for the host but not for his wife.

Conversation
Topics to avoid in conversation: politics, religion, and other controversial subjects.

Morocco

General Protocol
You should offer to remove your shoes before entering a Moroccan home, and you always should remove them when you enter a mosque.

Names/Greetings
Shaking hands is customary, although friends will usually greet by kissing.

Appointments/Punctuality
Prior appointments are advisable, although punctuality is seldom observed.

Hospitality/Gift Giving
Moroccan businessmen will invite you to their homes for huge feasts that last several hours, but you will rarely meet their wives.

You may wish to avoid lavishly complimenting your host on a possession, as he may feel socially obligated to give it to you.

Mozambique

Names/Greetings
First names are rarely used. Professional titles should be used if known.

Nigeria

General Protocol
Because of the wide range of customs and cultures among the ethnic peoples of Nigeria, a large variety of life-styles prevail.

Appointments/Punctuality
Prior appointments are important, especially with government officials.

Nigerians understand the Western habit of punctuality, although they generally are not too concerned about time. Because travel within Nigeria is difficult, allow plenty of time to reach your destination.

Conversation
One topic to avoid in conversation is religion.

Subjects suitable for discussion include their industrial achievements and plans for future development. Nigerians also enjoy discussing African politics, particularly their contributions to the OAU (Organization of African Unity), to ECOWAS (Economic Community of West African States), and to other African countries.

Senegal

Names/Greetings
It is customary to shake hands when introduced.

Appointments/Punctuality
Prior appointments are advisable. While punctuality is recommended, do not be surprised if your host is a bit late.

Hospitality/Gift Giving
Never eat food with the left hand, as this is considered offensive.

Conversation
Topics to be avoided: politics, government leaders, and religion.

Subjects suitable for discussion include the achievements and goals of the country, and its culture.

South Africa

General Protocol
South Africa is the industrial giant of Africa. It is a major producer of minerals including gold, diamonds, copper, and silver.

Most South Africans are bilingual, speaking English and Afrikaans (of Dutch origin).

There are very strict conventions and social rules in South Africa regarding race and color. Best to follow the lead of your host in regard to these particular areas.

Appointments/Punctuality
Prior appointments are necessary, and punctuality is strictly observed.

Conversation
South Africa is one of the few countries where it is difficult to avoid discussion of local politics and especially the evolving racial and social policies. And you will find residents divided on the subject.

Tanzania

Names/Greetings
It is customary to shake hands when being introduced. The verbal greeting *jambo* is also common.

Hospitality/Gift Giving
Gifts are often given by hosts at the time of departure from the country. At the same time visitors may reciprocate by presenting their hosts with a gift (but not flowers).

Conversation
Topics for discussion include the Tanzanian National Parks, African culture, and international politics.

Subjects to be avoided in conversation include the prevailing political climate.

Uganda

Names/Greetings
Handshaking is common.

Appointments/Punctuality
Prior appointments and punctuality are advisable.

Hospitality/Gift Giving
If you are invited to someone's home, it is polite, but not required, to take along a gift for your host or hostess. Wives are automatically included in invitations unless it is specified otherwise.

Conversation
Most topics can be discussed freely. National and world affairs and the arts are among the most popular topics.

Zambia

Names/Greetings
Handshaking, with the left hand supporting the right, is common. Use courtesy titles or, if known, professional titles.

Avoid direct eye contact with members of the opposite sex — it may suggest romantic overtures.

Appointments/Punctuality
A prior appointment is advisable, although it is no guarantee that the meeting will take place.

Hospitality/Gift Giving
At dinner you should ask for food, as it is considered impolite for the host to offer food first. It is also improper to refuse food.

Gifts should not be offered to government officials. Employees of state corporations may be embarrassed if offered an expensive item. Small gifts, perhaps bearing an imprint of your company, would be welcome.

Conversation
Avoid discussion of the shortage of items in the shops, local politics, or any inefficiencies you may have noted in the country.

Zambians like to discuss international politics.

The Middle East

Here are some general tips that the traveler will want to remember when visiting the countries of the Middle East.

General Protocol

Proper dress and proper decorum between the sexes are as important as observing any civil laws.

Islamic religious custom demands everything stop five times a day for prayers. While you are not expected to kneel or face Mecca, you must not interrupt or display impatience when your host does.

Whenever it is done gracefully, making a religious gesture toward an Arab is the sincerest form of flattery. It can be as simple as saying *Inshallah*, which means "God willing" and is used as commonly as "okay" is here.

Do not refer to the Persian Gulf. There it's the Arabian Gulf.

Muslims are never called Muhammadans.

Names/Greetings

Handshakes are customary outside the home, but a host may welcome you with a kiss on both cheeks and you should reciprocate.

Take an adequate supply of business cards. It may be appropriate to have one side printed in English and the other in the local language.

Appointments/Punctuality

Remember to respect Ramadan (the ninth month of the Islamic calendar). No work is done after noon during Ramadan.

The business week runs from Saturday to Wednesday or Thursday, with Thursday and/or Friday the Muslim day of rest and worship.

Punctuality is important for the visitor, although the host may not be on time.

Hospitality/Gift Giving

Even if an Arab invites you home, his wife (or wives) will probably not be seen (although she may well be in the kitchen supervising dinner). It is not polite to inquire about her (them), and if you do meet, be warm but undemonstrative. Do not even shake hands unless she takes the initiative, which she no doubt will not.

Do not ask for alcoholic drinks.

Pork meat and pigs are banned.

Be prepared to eat with your fingers if you see your host doing so. Eat with the right hand only.

Writing instruments make excellent gifts. People of the Middle East like the look of gold and they prefer fountain pens for the grace and flow of their alphabet.

Conversation
Avoid talk about your pet dog back home. Religion and politics are to be avoided in conversation.

It is safe to talk about the growth and development of the country visited.

Gestures
It is an insult to sit in such a way as to face your host with the soles of your shoes showing. Do not place your feet on a desk, table, or chair.

The Gulf States

The Gulf countries comprise Bahrain, Kuwait, Sultanate of Oman, Qatar, and the United Arab Emirates (UAE). The UAE is a country that comprises the following sheikdoms: Abu Dhabi, Ajman, Dubai, Fujaira, Ras al-Khaimah, Sharjah, and Umm al-Qaiwain.

General Protocol
The Gulf countries are located on the Arabian Gulf — it is important to *not* refer to that body of water as the Persian Gulf.

Names/Greetings
The customary greeting is: first, say *salaam alaykum*; next, shake hands while saying *kaif halak*; then, your host may place his left hand on your right shoulder and kiss you on both cheeks.

Appointments/Punctuality
While you must make prior appointments, don't be surprised to find several other businesspeople present and several meetings taking place at once.

Punctuality is important in Gulf countries.

Hospitality/Gift Giving
Skip a meal before dining at the home of an Arab businessman, so that you may show proper appreciation of the meal by eating copiously.

Your Arab host is likely to be very magnanimous. Be careful not to admire one of his possessions too warmly; he may insist on giving it to you, and you may be forced to accept rather than offend.

Gifts are appreciated but not expected. Avoid gifts of liquor and other items, such as photos and sculptures of women, which are prohibited by Islam.

**In the Arab countries, do not admire an object openly.
You may be the recipient of it.**

Conversation
Topics of particular interest in these countries are falcons and horses. Avoid conversations concerning Middle Eastern politics.

Gestures
If an Arab businessman takes your hand and holds it as you walk, do not be alarmed. He means it only as a sign of friendship.

Iran

Names/Greetings
A handshake accompanied by a slight bow is customary.
Visitors to Iran should address their hosts by their last name or by their academic rank or title.

Appointments/Punctuality
Most business meetings are by appointment. Business sessions respect punctuality, whereas for social engagements it is not that important.

Hospitality/Gift Giving
When invited to dinner, it is customary to bring a plant, flowers, or candy. It is also polite to decline an invitation a few times before accepting.

Conversation
Guests are the center of attention and are expected to be able to converse on many different topics.

Iraq

Appointments/Punctuality
Prior appointments are necessary. However, do not be disturbed if your host fails to show up on time.

Hospitality/Gift Giving
You will discover that in Iraq — unlike other Arab countries — alcoholic beverages are available.

Conversation
It is advisable to avoid discussions of religion or Middle Eastern politics.

Jordan

General Protocol
The sales approach should not be high-pressure, and you probably will be subjected to group-style business meetings with friends and other businessmen.

Appointments/Punctuality
Prior appointments are a must, but do not be disappointed if your host is not punctual.

Hospitality/Gift Giving
The host may ask a visitor to stay for dinner. It is customary to refuse twice before accepting.

Refuse seconds of any dish offered unless the host insists a couple of times, and even then accept only with a slight air of reluctance.

Flowers or sweets are customary gifts, but not alcohol.

Give polite but restrained thanks or praise; profuse praise can embarrass your host.

Conversation
Avoid any discussion of Middle Eastern politics. Other subjects to avoid in conversation: religion, family, and the large amount of U.S. aid.

Lebanon

Names/Greetings
Social amenities are serious business here. When greeting people, it is important to inquire about their well-being and their families.

Appointments/Punctuality
Punctuality is not especially important.

Hospitality/Gift Giving
Your host will try to make you feel as welcome as possible, as hospitality is the unspoken rule in Lebanon.

It is appropriate to talk about business only after the meal.

Politeness requires that you accept the coffee or tea you are offered.

Flowers or candy are welcome gifts. Gifts to be avoided include alcohol and cigarettes.

Conversation
The Lebanese appreciate compliments on such things as their homes, food, and achievements.

Subjects suitable for conversation include business, children, education, and travel. Or tell funny stories.

Topics to avoid include politics, religion, and sex.

Saudi Arabia

Names/Greetings
Customary greetings are elaborate. First, you say *salaam alaykum;*

second, you shake hands while saying *kaif halak*; next, a Saudi may extend his left hand to your right shoulder and kiss you on both cheeks.

If the Saudi is accompanied by a woman, do not expect to shake hands with her or even to be introduced.

Appointments/Punctuality
Prior appointments are necessary, but you may find several other businesspeople present and several meetings occurring simultaneously.

Punctuality is desirable in Saudi Arabia.

Hospitality/Gift Giving
When invited to the home of an Arab businessman for dinner, skip your previous meal so that you have a keen appetite. Proper appreciation of a meal is shown by eating large quantities.

If a dinner invitation includes a man's wife, she probably will be separated to go and eat with the other women.

There are no nightclubs and no movie theaters.

Be careful about admiring your host's watch, cuff links, or other possessions. An Arab businessman is often very magnanimous. He might give them to you on the spot and be offended if you refuse them.

Gifts are appreciated but not expected. Gifts to be avoided include liquor and items prohibited by Islam, such as photos and sculptures of women.

Conversation
Subjects to avoid in conversation include Middle Eastern politics and international oil politics.

Gestures
Do not pull your hand away sharply if an Arab businessman walking with you takes your hand and holds it as you go. This is a nice sign of friendship, nothing more.

Syria

Names/Greetings
Syrians often will greet visitors with a warm embrace and will inquire about their health. Women usually exchange kisses on either cheek.

Appointments/Punctuality
Prior appointments are necessary, but do not be disturbed if your contact does not arrive on time.

Do not be surprised if you arrive at a meeting to discover your host already occupied with someone else. It is common for

Arabs to discuss business with several friends and other businessmen at once.

Conversation
Subjects to avoid in conversation: Middle Eastern and international oil politics.

The Pacific and Asia

No region of the world has greater variety and diversity of languages, races, and religions than Asia, and the cultures of the countries of Asia and the Pacific have crisscrossed and intermingled for centuries.

General Protocol
Asians have an exquisite sense of politeness.

In most countries, particularly those in Southeast Asia, it is impolite to start talking business as soon as you sit down.

Although you might not receive clues from their outward appearance, you can be sure that your Asian counterparts are taking notice of yours — your behavior, your dress, the tailoring of your suit, the type of writing instrument you use.

Whatever happens, do not cause others to lose face. That's neither forgotten nor forgiven.

English is the language of commerce throughout Asia and the Pacific.

Names/Greetings
You should arrange to have business cards printed in English and the local language. Businesspeople will find they will use many cards during their visit to each country.

Appointments/Punctuality
Make appointments, keep them, and be punctual. However, do not be offended if others are late.

If you have a serious interest in developing business in this region, it is simply good business to read up on the country you are visiting and to know its culture and history.

Australia

General Protocol
Of all the countries in the region, Australia is probably the one in which Westerners, particularly Americans, feel the most comfortable.

Australians are direct, even by American standards, and tell it like it is. It is very difficult to impress an Australian and the effort is perhaps best not made.

One can approach most Australians, no matter how high their position, with the certainty of an attentive and cordial hearing. Any attempt to pull rank is resented.

Manual labor enjoys higher prestige in Australia than in America.

Australians are extremely informal in their rendering and receiving of personal services — a taxi driver expects a single male passenger to get in beside him.

While the Australians tend to dress more casually than their British counterparts, they are just as big on form and procedure, though the "rules" are very different.

Be sure you do not litter while in Australia, as visitors are expected to respect the Australians' high standards of cleanliness. Most Australians have a strong sense of community and tend to value collective effort highly.

Names/Greetings
People like to be given a firm handshake and called by their names. Men often call their friends "mate" as well.

Appointments/Punctuality
Prior appointments are necessary. Punctuality is highly regarded.

Hospitality/Gift Giving
It is acceptable to take flowers for the hostess or a bottle of wine when invited for lunch or dinner. When departing, be sure to thank your hosts for their hospitality.

Bangladesh

Names/Greetings
When introduced to a man, it is customary to shake hands. When introduced to a woman, wait for her to extend her hand first.

Appointments/Punctuality
Punctuality is highly regarded.

Hospitality/Gift Giving
You may be entertained in a hotel or club. It is customary for wives to accompany their husbands to such functions.

The People's Republic of China

General Protocol
You should refer to the country as the "People's Republic of China" or simply "China."

The Chinese consider tipping anyone an insult, although exceptions are starting to appear.

Names/Greetings
A slight bow is appropriate when meeting someone. A handshake is also acceptable. The Chinese are quite formal and will use the full title of guests during introductions.

Appointments/Punctuality
Prior appointments are necessary. Be prepared to wait a long time for Chinese businessmen to reach a decision.

Foreign businessmen usually find that their trip to China is highly organized and that punctuality is very important.

Hospitality/Gift Giving
A visit to a Chinese home is rare — unless the government has given prior approval.

Guests should plan to arrive a little early and should leave shortly after the meal. During the meal, be prepared with toasts expressing thanks, pleasure, and friendship.

It is polite to sample every dish, and when eating rice, it is customary to hold the bowl close to your mouth.

Business generally is not discussed during meals.

Gifts of any great value can cause embarrassment and usually are not accepted by the Chinese.

Conversation
Good topics for discussion include differences between China and the West, and the advances the Chinese have made.

Avoid mentioning Taiwan and do not criticize Chinese leadership.

Fiji

General Protocol
Respectful friendliness will take you a long way.

The custom is to remove your shoes when entering a house.

Names/Greetings
Fijians greet one another with a smile and raised eyebrows. Handshakes are appropriate.

Appointments/Punctuality
Punctuality is recommended, although day-to-day life is much more relaxed than in the West.

Hospitality/Gift Giving
Gifts are appreciated. It is courteous to drink at least a cup of kava when visiting. Refusal to drink kava with the people can start things off on the wrong foot.

Do not drop by a Fijian home without an invitation.

Be careful not to admire an object openly, as that might require the owner to give it to you.

Conversation
Be prepared to speak about personal experiences; displays of intellect do not go down very well.

Hong Kong

General Protocol
The people of Hong Kong are reserved and formal in almost all situations.

Avoid conflicts that would cause the Chinese to lose face.

Blue and white are the Chinese colors for mourning and should be avoided.

Have an abundant supply of business cards available — you'll use them often.

Names/Greetings
When greeting and leaving, handshakes are common. After the initial handshake business cards are presented with both hands.

Appointments/Punctuality
When appointments are made, a thirty-minute "courtesy time" often is allotted. However, businessmen are usually punctual.

Hospitality/Gift Giving
A guest will take a gift of fruit, candy, or cookies when invited to dinner and will present it to the hostess with both hands. Gifts to avoid: clocks, which symbolize death, and scissors or other sharp objects, which symbolize the severing of the relationship.

Never begin to eat or drink before your host does.

Gifts are exchanged at the time of Chinese New Year (at various dates from mid-January to February).

Conversation
To thank someone for a gift, say "DOR-jay;" for a service rendered the word is "Ng-GOI" (with the "ng" pronounced something like the "m" in "hmm").

Since the Chinese are delighted with Westerners who speak their language, a phrase in Cantonese will be greatly admired — but be very sure of your pronunciation.

Casual inquiries about health or business are considered polite conversation. One topic to avoid: the political situation in China.

India

General Protocol
Orthodox Sikhs wear a turban and do not smoke, eat beef, or cut their hair.

Remove your shoes before entering an Indian home.

Names/Greetings
Men may shake hands with other men when meeting or leaving. If introduced to a woman, a man should not shake hands but should place his palms together and bow slightly. Men should avoid touching a woman and should not talk to a lone woman in public.

Appointments/Punctuality
Punctuality is advisable.

Hospitality/Gift Giving
While orthodox Muslim women are usually kept from the view of men, husbands should be invited to bring their wives to a social function.

Upon arrival at an Indian home, you will be adorned with a garland of flowers, which you should remove immediately as a sign of humility.

Hindus do not eat any beef. The cow is a sacred animal.

Muslims do not eat pork and strict Muslims do not drink alcohol.

Always use your right hand to accept or pass food.

Guests may take gifts such as fruit and candy or they may take gifts for the children in the family.

Conversation
Indians enjoy conversation on cultural achievements, Indian traditions, other people, and foreign countries.

Avoid discussions of personal affairs and India's poverty, military expenditures, and huge amount of foreign aid.

Indonesia

General Protocol
Indonesian society is based on respect for the individual. This should be remembered in day-to-day affairs.

Shoes should be removed before entering carpeted rooms and holy places — especially mosques.

Business dealings are usually long, slow, and frustrating.

Names/Greetings
Handshaking and a nod of the head are proper when you are introduced for the first time.

Appointments/Punctuality
Punctuality is important but is never emphasized. Prior appointments are recommended.

Hospitality/Gift Giving
While visitors are not expected to eat only with the right hand, do not touch food with the left hand.

It is polite to take flowers when invited to dinner.

Indonesians generally do not expect gifts, but compliments and notes of appreciation are always welcome.

Gifts should be accepted graciously, since it is impolite to refuse anything.

Conversation
Avoid the subjects of local politics, socialism, and foreign aid.

Japan

General Protocol
Shoes are removed before entering a Japanese home but can be left on in a Western-style building.

Names/Greetings
The usual form of greeting is a long and low bow, not a handshake. Be prepared to exchange business cards.

Never address a Japanese by his first name. Only his family and very close friends use the first name.

To say "Mister (last name)," simply say the last name and add the word *san*.

Appointments/Punctuality
Punctuality is advisable for both business and social engagements.

Hospitality/Gift Giving
Visitors should be prepared to be invited by their business colleagues to lavish dinner parties, which may last for hours. These parties are almost always held in Japanese restaurants or nightclubs.

Entertainment of visitors at private homes is not very common. If you do visit a Japanese home, remove your hat and gloves once inside the entrance to the house and then remove your shoes. It is not customary to take flowers for the hostess, but take a box of cakes or candy.

Never surprise your Japanese guest with a gift.
He may not be in a position to reciprocate immediately.

If you are offered a gift, thank the person and wait for one or two more offers before accepting it. Receive the gift with both hands.

The Japanese enjoy receiving gifts, which should be wrapped in pastel-colored paper, no bows. They particularly relish gifts of brandy and frozen steaks. Gifts given in twos are supposed to bring good luck, so such things as cuff]inks and pen and pencil sets are especially well received. Never give four of anything, as one Japanese word for four is also the word for death.

Conversation
One topic to be avoided: World War II.

Malaysia

General Protocol
Before entering a mosque or a home (especially one belonging to the Malays, who make up the country's largest ethnic group), remove your shoes and sunglasses.

Kuala Lumpur, the capital city, has harsh penalties against littering, so be careful where you drop that cigarette butt.

Bahasa Malaysia is the national language, but English is widely spoken, especially in commerce.

Names/Greetings
The handshake is a common form of greeting between men, but a slight bow or nod would be more appropriate between men and Malaysian women — especially women of the older generation. Also, have your business card ready.

Appointments/Punctuality
Prior appointments are advisable. Punctuality is expected but not emphasized.

Hospitality/Gift Giving
Malaysians are generally friendly and cordial toward foreign visitors. Entertainment is an important part of business arrangements and usually takes the form of lunch or dinner at a restaurant.

At Muslim dinners never use the left hand to touch food. Follow the lead of the host to be sure. Muslims do not eat pork or drink alcoholic beverages. Hindus and some Buddhists do not eat beef. Traditionally, the Malays and the Indians eat with their hands. Chinese eat with chopsticks and a spoon.

Gift-giving customs vary among the cultures: Chinese, Malay, and Indian. But no matter what ethnic group the recipient belongs to, it is always considered impolite to present a gift with the left hand or to open a gift immediately.

If you are presented with a gift, a note of appreciation is in order.

Conversation
Subjects most Malaysians like to talk about include general affairs, family, sports, and food.

New Zealand

General Protocol
Tipping is not common, and a tip often will be refused.

Be prepared to be formal until a more relaxed atmosphere has been established.

Names/Greetings
Shake hands on meeting and leaving. Wait for women to offer their hand first.

Appointments/Punctuality
Prior appointments are advisable and visitors should try to be a bit early.

Hospitality/Gift Giving
Visitors usually invite customers to lunch at a hotel or restaurant. Otherwise, business meetings will be at the host's office. If you are invited to a New Zealander's home for a meal, you could take a modest gift of chocolates or wine, although it is not compulsory.

Conversation
New Zealanders like to talk about national and international politics, the weather, and sports. They appreciate visitors who have an understanding of their culture.

One topic to avoid is racial issues. Do not include New Zealand as part of Australia or "Australasia."

Pakistan

Names/Greetings
The common greeting is the handshake. Close friends may embrace. A man should not shake hands with a woman or touch her in public.

Use last name and title when addressing a Pakistani.

Appointments/Punctuality
Although Pakistanis are not time conscious, they will expect their Western visitors to arrive on time.

Most businesses are closed on Fridays.

Hospitality/Gift Giving
It is not unusual for a man to be invited to dinner without his

wife. Even if the wife is invited to dinner, a man often will come alone.

Many of the traditional foods are eaten by hand and it is important to use only the right hand when eating.

While the Pakistanis are forbidden to eat pork, they enjoy beef, lamb, and poultry. The use of alcoholic beverages is not encouraged.

It is impolite to discuss business at dinner.

Conversation
It is advisable to avoid discussion of politics.

The Philippines

General Protocol
Americans and Europeans usually feel at home in the Philippines, where the culture is cosmopolitan and reflects years of Spanish and American influences. Americans are generally well liked and the American life-style is emulated. English is the language of government, business, and education.

Names/Greetings
The everyday greeting for acquaintances is a handshake with men and women, and occasionally a pat on the back for men.

Appointments/Punctuality
It is advisable to be punctual.

Hospitality/Gift Giving
Filipinos are extremely hospitable — an overnight guest, for example, will often be assigned the master bedroom.

If a gift is given — such as flowers — it is given on arrival. It is also customary to send a gift or thank-you note the day after a dinner or other social gathering.

During dinner, the best compliment you can give your host is to eat heartily.

Conversation
Topics to avoid are politics, religion, local conditions, corruption, and foreign aid.

Filipinos are extremely family-oriented and conversation about their family is usually welcome.

Samoa

General Protocol
It is customary to remove one's shoes before entering a Samoan home. Visitors should not enter a home until mats have been placed on the floor. They will sit cross-legged on the mats.

Names/Greetings
A formal greeting is usually given before a business meeting begins. Samoans prize eloquence, however, so it's best to have a speech prepared.

Hospitality/Gift Giving
Even though fingers are used when eating in a Samoan home, in most cases visitors will be provided with utensils.

The kava ceremony is a sacred and highly respected custom in Samoa. If served kava, before you start drinking, hold the cup out in front of you and spill a few drops.

Guests will usually receive a gift and should be prepared to give one in return.

Gestures
Avoid pointing your legs toward the center of the room.

Singapore

General Protocol
Shoes are removed before one enters a mosque and sometimes before one enters a home.

Streets and other places are kept wonderfully clean due to harsh penalties against littering. So watch where you drop that cigarette butt.

Names/Greetings
Due to the British influence, Singapore is quite Westernized. However, the customs of the many ethnic groups are also followed, so greetings vary.

The handshake is the most common greeting — with a slight bow to the Orientals.

Appointments/Punctuality
Western visitors are expected to be punctual. Prior appointments are advisable.

Hospitality/Gift Giving
Entertainment usually takes the form of a lunch or dinner.

Do not use your left hand when eating with a Malay or an Indian.

Should you be invited to a Singapore home for dinner, a box of chocolates or flowers would be appreciated.

Conversation
Topics to avoid in conversation include religion and politics. And never make humorous remarks about the food being served.

Subjects that are acceptable to discuss are travel experiences, news of countries visited, and economic advances in Singapore.

South Korea

General Protocol
Avoid talking or laughing loudly in any situation. Koreans, especially the women, cover their mouths when laughing.

Women's liberation has not been accepted yet. Men go through doors first. Women help men with their coats.

Blowing your nose in front of others is considered bad manners.

Shoes are always removed before entering a Korean home or restaurant.

Names/Greetings
Men greet each other by bowing slightly and shaking hands with both hands or with the right hand. Women usually do not shake hands.

Family names come first, then the given name. It is difficult to distinguish male from female names in Korea.

Appointments/Punctuality
Prior appointments are necessary and, while punctuality is not of great importance, Westerners are usually expected to arrive on time.

Hospitality/Gift Giving
Business entertainment is considered very important and is usually limited to restaurants and bars. Wives are rarely included.

All courses of a meal are served at once.

If you are invited to a Korean home, it would be appropriate to take flowers or a small gift, to be offered with both hands. Gifts are not opened in front of the giver.

Conversation
Avoid discussions of socialism, communism, internal politics, and criticism of the government.

Sri Lanka

General Protocol
Visitors should be aware of the various religious restrictions, especially those concerning food, observed by the different castes.

Names/Greetings
Because of the strong influence of the British, English greetings are suitable. It is proper to address people by title.

Appointments/Punctuality
Prior appointments are necessary. It is considered polite to respect punctuality.

Hospitality/Gift Giving
Sri Lankans are hospitable and courteous. It is the usual custom for them to offer visitors tea at the beginning of a meeting. Tea is the national drink.

Tahiti

General Protocol
Tahitian custom calls for removing one's shoes before entering a home.

Names/Greetings
Most people shake hands when they meet, and if you are in a group of thirty or less, you are expected to shake hands with everyone. Tahitians usually kiss each other on the cheeks when greeting.

Hospitality/Gift Giving
If invited to a Tahitian home, you should express interest in your host's home and family. But be careful — your Tahitian host might make a gift of a prized possession if you express too great an interest in it.

Tahitian food is eaten with the fingers, but table manners depend greatly on the family's customs. Observe your host and do as he does.

Taiwan

General Protocol
Taiwanese businessmen can take a long time, by American standards, to reach a decision, so be patient.

Shoes are not worn in some homes (slippers are substituted). Observe your host.

Names/Greetings
A handshake is customary when meeting acquaintances and close friends. A nod of the head is appropriate when meeting someone for the first time. A *slight* bow shows respect, but it should not be overdone.

Appointments/Punctuality
If you arrive at your appointment shortly before or after the scheduled time, that is perfectly acceptable.

Hospitality/Gift Giving
Entertainment is usually offered in restaurants and not in the home.

Taiwanese meals are elaborate and exhausting. Be prepared to eat sparingly during the early stages of what could be a twenty-course meal. Toasts are common; *kampai* means "bottoms up."

Chopsticks and a ceramic spoon are the common eating utensils in Taiwan.

A small gift, such as fruit, candy, or cookies, is appropriate when visiting a family at home. Both hands should be used when handing a gift or other object to another person. Thank-you notes are a must and are appreciated.

Conversation
Avoid discussing mainland China and local politics.

Thailand

General Protocol
It is customary to remove your shoes when entering a Thai home. Avoid stepping on doorsills, where Thai tradition says a spirit resides.

Never touch a person's head — even a child's — as the head is regarded the highest part of the body, both literally and figuratively. Similarly, if you watch Thais at a social gathering, you'll notice that young people go to considerable lengths to keep their heads lower than those of older people, to avoid giving the impression of "looking down" on them. This isn't always possible, of course, but it's the effort that counts.

Public displays of affection between men and women are frowned upon.

Displays of temper, especially in public, are considered poor manners.

Thai businessmen take a long time to reach a decision. Be patient.

Names/Greetings
Thais do not usually shake hands except in more Westernized social groups. The traditional and most common Thai greeting — the *wai* — is made by placing both hands together in a prayer position at the chest and bowing slightly. Generally, a younger person *wais* an older, who returns the gesture.

Don't be surprised if you are addressed by your first name — for instance, "Mr. Bob" or "Miss Mary" — instead of your surname.

Appointments/Punctuality
Prior appointments are necessary and punctuality is a sign of courtesy.

Hospitality/Gift Giving
Guests should show interest in the host's family and house but should not compliment one object too greatly, as the host might feel obliged to make a gift of it.

Normally, small souvenirs make acceptable gifts. Gifts usually should be wrapped. Flowers make suitable gifts.

Conversation
Topics to avoid in conversation include politics, the royal family, and religion.

Gestures
Never point to anything casually with your foot. When standing or seated, never angle your foot in such a way that it is conspicuous or that the sole is visible.

Tonga

Names/Greetings
Handshaking and a spoken greeting are customary.

Tongans usually call people by their first name, unless they wish to show special respect, in which case they use the title and family name together.

Hospitality/Gift Giving
While utensils are often used at the table, Tongans prefer to eat with their hands.

The family will appreciate your sitting on the floor mats in their home.

Gifts are appropriate but are expected only from close friends. Flowers are not regarded as gifts.

Central and South America

It is important to recognize diversity in Latin America. Customs, phrases, and behavior may not be the same in Argentina as in Colombia. There are some fairly safe generalizations, though, and here are some of them.

General Protocol
Latin Americans tend to stand close during conversation. If you want to do business in this part of the world, learn to accept your host's distance.

Tipping varies according to country.

Names/Greetings
In much of Central and South America, the custom is to shake hands both on arrival and departure.

Arrange to have business cards printed in English and the local language.

Appointments/Punctuality
As for punctuality, a thirty-minute delay is customary.

Hospitality/Gift Giving
Latin Americans are warm and friendly people. They enjoy entertaining.

The main meal of the day is at noon throughout Latin America.

It is customary to give gifts. Appropriate gifts for women include perfume and name brand items; for men, novelties or men's accessories, also name brands; for both, unique items with an art/history relationship from your homeland.

When you are invited to a home for dinner, flowers or good wine and liquors make suitable gifts. Toasts are common, but let the host say his first, then be prepared with your own.

Dress
Wear proper attire (jacket and tie) even if the climate is warmer than that to which you are accustomed.

Conversation
Topics for conversation could include mention of local folklore customs, historic dates, or heroes.

Argentina

Names/Greetings
Men, when meeting after a long absence, hug each other (abrazo). Women will shake hands with both hands and kiss each other on the cheek. However, when meeting someone for the first time, a simple handshake and a nod of the head will do.

Appointments/Punctuality
Prior appointments are necessary.

Hospitality/Gift Giving
Gifts to be avoided include personal items such as ties and shirts.

If a visitor is entertained in an Argentine home, he should arrange to send flowers or candy to his hostess.

A guest should wait for the host to sit down before sitting, and to open the door for him before leaving.

Conversation
Argentines welcome compliments about their children, the meal, and their home.

Avoid discussion of controversial subjects such as politics and religion. If women are present at dinner, refrain from discussing business matters.

Feel free to talk about sports — particularly soccer — and the beauty of the local parks and gardens.

Bolivia

Names/Greetings
Handshakes are common. If the person's hand is dirty, his arm will be offered to shake instead. Bolivians often greet friends and acquaintances with a spoken salutation.

Appointments/Punctuality
Visitors should be punctual, even if others are late.

Hospitality/Gift Giving
Bolivians expect visitors to eat everything on their plate. Therefore, you should take a small portion of each type of food offered.

Be judicious when complimenting the food during dinner, as your praise probably will invite a second helping.

Flowers and small gifts are usually given to the host. Gifts are customarily opened after the giver has left.

Entertainment for businessmen is normally a luncheon or dinner in a restaurant. Wives do not normally attend such events.

Conversation
Your attempts to use Spanish will be appreciated.

Generally, any subject can be discussed, although it would be well to avoid politics and religion.

Brazil

General Protocol
Remember, Portuguese is the language of Brazil.

Names/Greetings
Brazilians feel no shame in showing their emotions and will embrace on the street. Men and women always shake hands

upon meeting and leaving. When women meet, they exchange kisses by placing their cheeks together and kissing the air.

When leaving a small group, be sure to shake hands with everyone present.

Appointments/Punctuality
Brazilians, like most Latin Americans, are casual about both time and work. In fact, it is customary to arrive ten or fifteen minutes late for an appointment.

Never start right into business discussions unless your host does so first.

Hospitality/Gift Giving
Expect to be frequently served small cups of very strong coffee.

If a visitor has been entertained in a home, it is polite to send flowers to the hostess the next day, with a thank-you note. Be sure the flowers are not purple (a sign of death).

Conversation
Brazilians are very proud of their children and appreciate your attention to them. Brazilian men love good jokes and love to laugh, but avoid ethnic jokes and do not discuss Argentina. Also avoid discussions of politics, religion, and other controversial subjects.

Chile

Names/Greetings
When people are first introduced, a handshake is customary, as is a kiss on the right cheek. Male Chileans may greet each other with hearty abrazos (hugs), with women customarily kissing each other on the cheek.

Appointments/Punctuality
Prior appointments are necessary and Chilean businessmen respect punctuality. Meetings should start *and* end on time.

Hospitality/Gift Giving
Business entertaining generally is done at major hotels and restaurants.

When visiting a home, guests should wait outside the door until invited inside.

A gift of a bouquet of flowers to the hostess is appropriate.

Conversation
Business discussions should be preceded by some light conversation.

Don't go native.

Topics to be avoided in conversation include local politics and religion. Chileans are pleased if guests show an interest in their family and especially in their children.

Colombia

General Protocol
Colombian businessmen prefer slow deliberations and like quiet discussions over black Colombian coffee before any business is transacted.

Be sure to plan to relax your first day in Bogotá — the altitude may affect you.

Names/Greetings
A handshake is the customary greeting. Men will shake hands with everyone when entering a home or group and also when leaving. Women do not usually shake hands with other women; they clasp forearms.

Use title and last name when addressing a Colombian.

Appointments/Punctuality
Strict punctuality is not a must anywhere in Colombia, although being on time is somewhat more important in the larger cities.

Hospitality/Gift Giving
When a visitor is invited to a home, it is customary to send a gift of fruit, flowers, or chocolates before arrival, if time permits. If not, send a gift afterward, with a thank-you note.

Gifts should not be personal unless you know the person very well. Then you may give a tie to a man and perfume to a woman.

Conversation
The Colombians will appreciate your interest in sports (particularly soccer), art, Colombian coffee, and the beauty of the countryside.

Bullfighting is popular in Colombia and Colombians would resent any adverse comments from visitors.

Avoid political discussions.

Gestures
It is impolite to yawn in public.

Costa Rica

Names/Greetings
When greeting, men always shake hands; women who are friends or relatives kiss each other once on the cheek.

Appointments/Punctuality
If an uninvited visitor drops by, he may be refused admittance.

Hospitality/Gift Giving
People frequently exchange gifts on all kinds on special occasions.

Ecuador

General Protocol
Relax on your first day in Ecuador. You may have trouble breathing until you become accustomed to the high altitude.

Most stores close at siesta time, which lasts about two hours.

Names/Greetings
The handshake is used when meeting someone for the first time. Women who are close friends kiss each other, and men embrace.

Hospitality/Gift Giving
A visitor compliments new things in the home. After a meal in the home, each visitor should thank the host or hostess profusely. Lavish thanks are also called for when receiving a gift.

Conversation
It is advisable to avoid political topics and any issues that imply the superiority of the U.S.

El Salvador

General Protocol
It is not polite for someone from the U.S. to introduce himself as an American. Salvadorans are also American.

Names/Greetings
Handshaking is the usual form of greeting, although some people merely nod when meeting.

Only close acquaintances use first names or the surname alone. The use of titles shows respect.

Visitors should show particular respect when addressing the elderly.

Hospitality/Gift Giving
A guest should compliment the person who has prepared the food — and especially compliment the hostess.

Small gifts are commonly exchanged, but elaborate or expensive gifts are often considered inappropriate.

Gestures
Do not be alarmed if a Salvadoran puts his arm around you, as this is simply a sign of friendship.

Guatemala

Names/Greetings
It is appropriate to shake hands when meeting someone and to say something in Spanish, if possible. Men greet each other with a handshake, and close friends embrace and pat each other on the back. Close women friends usually give a gentle hug and a kiss on the cheek.

Hospitality/Gift Giving
Dinner guests may take small gifts such as flowers or candy.
    It is advisable to discuss business affairs outside the home and away from the family.

Conversation
Expressing admiration of personality is a key to gaining respect.
    Avoid criticizing the country, and especially avoid criticism of individual Guatemalans, as they probably will physically defend their honor.

Honduras

General Protocol
Machismo — the idea that men are superior to women — prevails.

Names/Greetings
Close acquaintances often greet each other with a hearty hug (abrazo). Otherwise, a handshake is sufficient. Women who know each other often exchange a kiss on the cheek.
    It is best to use a person's official title and last name at first meeting.

Hospitality/Gift Giving
Hondurans are especially hospitable, and you can expect to be invited to a meal. Gifts are not required, but respectful thanks should be given to the family.

Mexico

General Protocol
Mexico City's high altitude, smog, and wild traffic should be

respected and anticipated — and, to compound the problem, unless care is taken about drinking water, the visitor may suffer diarrhea, commonly called Montezuma's revenge. All this is negated, however, by a friendly, gracious, and easygoing business atmosphere.

Names/Greetings
Handshakes are customary. However, longtime friends may engage in a full embrace — the abrazo. Women often greet each other with a kiss on the cheek.

Appointments/Punctuality
The two- or three-hour midday siesta is a bad time for business appointments.

Hospitality/Gift Giving
While it is not customary to take gifts, they are appreciated. Gifts may be wrapped and presented as you would in the U.S.

Flowers are not expected by host or hostess. If you do send flowers, remember that for some classes of Mexicans yellow flowers connote death, red flowers cast spells, and white ones lift the spells. Thank-you notes are not common but are appreciated.

Conversation
Mexicans appreciate a visitor's efforts to speak Spanish.

Avoid historical and political topics, such as the Mexican-American War and illegal aliens.

Safe topics include the weather, fashion, travel, art, and the parks and museums.

Nicaragua

General Protocol
Machismo — the concept that men are superior to women — prevails.

Names/Greetings
When meeting someone, it is appropriate to smile, shake hands, and say a greeting (in Spanish, if possible). Men greet each other with a handshake. Close friends embrace and pat each other on the back. Women usually give a gentle hug and kiss each other on the cheek.

Hospitality/Gift Giving
Dinner guests may take small gifts such as flowers or candy.

Conversation
Nicaraguans appreciate polite inquiries into their health and family.

Compliments on personality are more appreciated than compliments on possessions.

Panama

General Protocol
Americans who do not mingle with the local people are considered cold and aloof.

Machismo — the concept that men are superior to women — prevails.

Names/Greetings
Friends nod and embrace when they meet. A handshake is appropriate among business associates.

Appointments/Punctuality
Punctuality is held in very little regard here, and meetings usually start later than scheduled. It is impolite to set a time for meetings to end.

Hospitality/Gift Giving
Food or seedlings are appropriate as gifts when visiting the interior of Panama. In the urban areas no gift is necessary, as the favor of giving the guest dinner is expected to be reciprocated.

Conversation
Avoid discussion of local politics and the former Canal Zone.

Paraguay

Names/Greetings
When people first meet, the greeting *mucho gusto* is often used. People stand very close when conversing and men often embrace on meeting. Women usually kiss each other on both cheeks. Close friends may walk arm in arm.

A visitor should refrain from using first names until invited to do so.

Appointments/Punctuality
Although your Paraguayan counterpart may be late, you are expected to be punctual.

Hospitality/Gift Giving
When visiting a home, the guest usually greets the host with a short, formal speech and asks permission to enter.

Conversation
Topics suitable for conversation include the family, sports, current events, and the weather. Paraguayans are very proud of their hydroelectric dams.
It is not advisable to discuss politics.

Peru

General Protocol
The Peruvians are conversative, formal, and proud of their Incan and Spanish colonial backgrounds.

Names/Greetings
Men and women shake hands when meeting and parting. Men often greet close friends with a hug (the abrazo). Close women friends often greet each other with a kiss on the cheek. A pat on the back is a polite way to greet a youth.

Hospitality/Gift Giving
Gifts of flowers are appropriate for any occasion.
Most dinner invitations are for 9 P.M. — or later. It is considered correct to arrive a half hour after the stated time for dinner. The only event that requires absolute punctuality is a bullfight.
During dinner, politeness requires a guest to eat everything on his plate or to politely excuse himself.

Conversation
All topics except local politics are acceptable.

Uruguay

Names/Greetings
Handshaking is the usual way of greeting. First names are used only between close friends.

Appointments/Punctuality
Meetings are extremely formal but rarely start on time. If you are a few minutes late, you will not be criticized.

Hospitality/Gift Giving
While most entertaining is done in restaurants, a visitor may be invited to an Uruguayan's home. Remember to send flowers or chocolates to your hostess before the occasion.

Conversation
Avoid the subject of politics. Communism is a very sensitive subject and should not be mentioned.

Uruguayans like to talk about sports — especially soccer.

Venezuela

Names/Greetings
Men greet each other with a hug and women greet each other with an embrace and a kiss on the cheek. Handshaking is also common.

People stand very close together when talking.

Appointments/Punctuality
The average Venezuelan businessman is very busy. You should be prepared to be punctual and to get directly to the point in discussions.

Hospitality/Gift Giving
Visitors should never sit at the head of the table, as those seats are reserved for the mother and father of the family.

Venezuelans usually invite only special close friends to their homes. Flowers sent to the host or hostess before an event will be appreciated. Otherwise, take flowers or candy when you arrive — or send a thank-you note after the event.

An appropriate gift for a man is something for the office — such as a good-quality pen. A woman would appreciate the gift of an orchid — the national flower.

The Caribbean

The Caribbean area comprises independent countries as well as territories that presently are or formerly were closely associated with Great Britain, France, Holland, and the United States. There are a wide variety of races, languages, and cultures. A visitor to the Caribbean area may want to keep in mind the following general tips.

General Protocol
While English is the prevailing language, other languages include Spanish, French, Dutch, and several dialects.

Names/Greetings
Generally, people shake hands when meeting and parting.

Visitors should be prepared to have a supply of business cards printed in English and the local language (if other than English).

Appointments/Punctuality
Prior appointments are advisable. Punctuality is not closely adhered to in the region.

Hospitality/Gift Giving
Table manners are very informal.

Dress
Casual warm-weather clothing is acceptable in most areas.

Conversation
While it is acceptable to discuss the economy, the tourist business, and the weather, it is advisable to avoid discussing local politics, religion, and controversial subjects, particularly race.

Haiti

General Protocol
French is spoken in Haiti.

At 8 A.M. and 6 P.M., a bugle is played and a flag raised. If in the vicinity — either on foot or in a car — you are expected to stop, get out of the car, and stand respectfully.

Hospitality/Gift Giving
It is not necessary to take a gift on the first trip, but a gift should be taken on the second visit. The gift may be of modest value — something unusual from the U.S. would be appreciated.

Conversation
Avoid political discussions. The rare beauty of Haitian native art is a safe and easy topic.

Puerto Rico

Names/Greetings
People shake hands when they meet. Often, close friends embrace. Women may grasp each other's shoulders and kiss on the cheek.

People stand very close when talking — and moving away could be considered an insult.

Hospitality/Gift Giving
Gifts are given freely and they are unwrapped immediately when received. It is polite to decline anything offered a few times before accepting.

A guest should stay for conversation after a meal is over.

Conversation
Visitors who attempt to speak some Spanish are appreciated, but almost all Puerto Ricans speak English.

Puerto Ricans object to open criticism, "pushiness," and greed.

Puerto Ricans appreciate discussing their cultural heritage and their rapid economic growth. But statehood with the U.S. is a hotly debated and divisive issue.

North America

Canada

Canada maintains strong links with Great Britain, other European countries, and its neighbor to the south, the United States. A large part of the population is French-speaking. Two largely unknown facts: Canada is the second largest country in the world, and it is the largest trading partner of the United States.

General Protocol
Remember that Canada is made up of many different ethnic groups, and while customs generally are similar throughout the country, there are some differences. As always, the best rule is to follow your host's lead.

Canadians are somewhat more conservative than U.S. citizens.

Names/Greetings
Shaking hands at meeting and parting is appropriate.

Appointments/Punctuality
Punctuality is expected in most of Canada.

Hospitality/Gift Giving
Most entertaining is done in restaurants and clubs.

If you are entertained in a private home, it would be courteous to take or send flowers to your hostess. Avoid sending white lilies; they are associated with funerals.

Conversation
In conversation avoid taking sides on partition — separation into separate states, French-speaking and English-speaking.

Canadians are proud of their country and take exception to exaggerated comparisons with the U.S.

Mentioning positive examples and making favorable comments about the people and their country are most welcome.

CHAPTER 3

Gift Giving
and
Receiving

Rules for business gift giving in the U.S. are simple:

- **Lavish, extravagant gifts are definitely out.** Ever since President Eisenhower's chief aide, Sherman Adams, generated a national scandal in the 1950s by accepting a pricey vicuna coat as a gift from a lobbyist, American businesspeople have shown restraint when presenting and receiving gifts. Furthermore, the Internal Revenue Service allows only twenty-five dollars per gift to qualify for a deduction as a business expense. Anything more than that must go right to the bottom line.

- **Put your company name on, in, or at least near the gift.** After all, the whole object is to make the recipient remember who gave the gift.

- **Wrapping** a business gift is not necessary.

An appropriate alternate to a gift is to take the deserving person to dinner, or to an entertainment or sporting event.

Simple. The American way is direct, efficient, and the *"right"* way. End of chapter, right?

Sorry. As you've paged through this book, you've come to appreciate that the axis of the world does not run downward through the American continent, the earth does not revolve around us and our customs, and ours is not necessarily the only way or the right way.

In fact, once we *leave* the U.S., there can be oceans of difference between the proper protocols for gift giving.

Many Americans have learned this the hard way.

Examples:

A Grand Rapids, Michigan, export manager once entertained a group of valued Japanese customers. Knowing the Japanese propensity for gift giving, the American placed a small, boxed gift near each place setting at the dinner table. He had chosen a small Swiss penknife as his gift. After the group was seated, he insisted the guests open their presents. (Mistake number one, as we'll learn later in this chapter.) Each guest reluctantly opened his package, and the American executive was greeted with a stony silence. (Mistake number two: presenting a knife to a Japanese is symbolically suggesting suicide.)

In China, avoid the gift of a clock.
To the older generation, a clock is a symbol of bad luck.

A West Virginia executive, visiting Germany for the first time, was invited to the home of his largest customer. He decided to be gallant and bring his hostess a bouquet of flowers. (So far, so good.) He selected a dozen red roses. (Oops! Terrible mistake.) He later learned that in Germany, first, it is bad luck to present an even number of flowers, and second, red roses are symbolic of a strong romantic interest. He was making what amounted to a pass at his customer's wife.

Other reported gift-giving gaffes:

Handing a bottle of booze to a devout Muslim.

Giving products decorated with cowhide in India, where cows are considered sacred.

Taking toys made in mainland China to the children of a business associate in Taiwan.

Even U.S. presidents are not errorproof. When Lyndon Johnson received a gift from the president of Mexico, he found he had nothing to give in return. From that day forward he had his Secret Service agents carry a supply of Accutron watches in order to avoid a similar embarrassment. George Bush once gave Chinese Premier Li Peng a pair of black cowboy boots, with one boot displaying the Chinese flag and the other the Stars and Stripes. In Asia the sole of the foot is considered the lowliest, dirtiest part of the body, so mixing flag and foot was hardly diplomatic.

In this chapter we will pinpoint those parts of the world where gift giving is a heavy part of the culture and identify where — as in the U. S. — the rules are fairly lightweight. We will also provide a list of ideas, or thought-starters, for *good* gifts around the world.

This information has been collected by the editor of this book over the past five years from varied sources: 1) personal visits to many of the countries cited, 2) careful screening of other travel and etiquette books, some not yet available in the U.S., and 3) conversations with scores of veteran international travelers. (Note: The editor presents between thirty and forty programs and seminars per year on international protocol and behavior. Happily, many audience members relate their mistakes, as well as their advice, when it comes to gift-giving practices around the world.)

So, take a tip from scores of other world-wise, gift-bearing travelers who have followed in their footsteps, and learn the lore of gift giving, whether you are traveling afar or hosting at home.

We begin this gift-giving globe-trot with a **ladder chart** showing where the presentation of gifts is a high art form and where it is just a lowly ho hum.

Top Rung:

Japan
It stands alone atop the ladder. Gift giving is ingrained in the Japanese culture. You'll find more commentary on this — much more — later in this chapter.

Middle of the Ladder:

Middle East
By American standards Middle Easterners can be embarrassingly gracious and generous, The roots for such generosity are found in the nomad tradition of offering hospitality to strangers and friends alike.

Pacific Rim countries (Korea, Taiwan, Hong Kong, China, Malaysia, Thailand)
Perhaps not as extreme or ritualistic about gift giving as the Japanese, but not far behind.

Latin American countries
Gifts are frequently exchanged, but they are not considered a necessity.

The Lower Rungs:
(countries where business gift giving is conducted, but if you should overlook presenting a gift, you won't be deported.)

Australia
Canada
United States
United Kingdom
Northern European countries (Scandinavia, Germany, Belgium, the Netherlands)
Central and Eastern Europe (the former Soviet Union countries, Austria, Bulgaria, Hungary, Romania, the Czech Republic, the Slovak Republic, Albania, and Poland)
Southern Europe (Italy, Spain, France, Switzerland, Portugal, Greece, and Turkey)

Now, let's examine each of these in detail.

Country-By-Country Customs

Japan

An American woman living in Wisconsin volunteered to tutor English to a Japanese woman who had moved into the same community. "Before each lesson, and on each and every visit," the American reported, "the Japanese lady brought me a gift — a book, some paper sculpture, flowers, or candy. It was embarrassing."

Unknowingly, this American was experiencing a vestige of protocol rooted centuries deep in the Japanese culture.

Gift giving is an institution and a revered custom in Japan. According to Business Tokyo magazine, among the Japanese "gift giving is a necessity, not merely a nicety as in the West."

In Japan the proper gift is thought to express the giver's true friendship, gratitude, and respect far better than words can. And among the Japanese those three qualities rank right up there with three more: honesty, integrity, and loyalty.

According to Boye De Menthe, author and expert on etiquette in Japan, specific gift-giving prescriptions have prevailed in Japanese society for centuries. They spell out the type of gift to give and how gifts should be wrapped. Even the precise method of presentation is carefully spelled out. In fact, in the past wealthy Japanese families had one member of the family or staff whose primary responsibility was to advise family members on gift-giving protocol.

Today there are numerous occasions when the Japanese give gifts among themselves and to foreigners residing in Japan. Two of these are *oseibo*, toward the end of the year, and *O-chugen*, at midyear. According to John C. Condon, in his fine book *With Respect to the Japanese* (Intercultural Press, Yarmouth, Me., 1984), these are occasions when the Japanese may give gifts to their doctors, teachers, or others whom they wish to thank for past and continued kindnesses. These are also the times when companies pass out huge cash bonuses.

It does not take a special holiday or season, however, for the Japanese to present gifts. A simple business visit, whether here or there, is also an occasion for gift giving. So if you plan to visit Japan or to have Japanese visit you here, be prepared.

Following is a detailed set of rules for gift giving with the Japanese. But don't panic. You won't be hurled off Mount Fuji for violations. Westerners are not expected to know them all.

However, if you want to impress your Japanese counterpart in a country where form and style count just as much as substance, here is what you should know and do.

Never surprise the receiver. Toward the end of your visit, quietly alert the recipient that you have a small memento. If the gift is for an individual, present it to him in private; if it is a group gift, indicate this in advance so that the group can be assembled. The worst offense would be to present a gift to one individual and ignore others who may be present.

Wrap the gift. Don't use white paper, because white is associated with death. Don't use brightly colored papers or bows. If you buy your gifts at a Japanese department store, they will automatically be wrapped. If you have brought unwrapped gifts with you, it's likely your hotel can provide a gift-wrapping service. Also, a wrapped gift is often carried inside a shopping bag to avoid ostentatiousness and to minimize any hint that a gift is being conveyed.

Don't insist that the receiver open the gift then and there. As Condon explains, "the gift will not be opened until later, away from the eyes of the giver. There are several reasons for this, including not wanting any tinge of disappointment or puzzlement on the face of the recipient to leak out." Also, if several gifts are being presented to different people of different stature, opening them later avoids any possible comparisons.

Give and receive gifts with both hands. This is merely viewed as a gesture of respect and humility.

Comment on the modesty and insignificance of your gift. Again, this conveys humility. Even the most lavish gift presented by the Japanese will be accompanied by the phase *tsumaranai mon*, which means "uninteresting or dull thing." This perhaps sounds excessively modest, but it is actually sending a separate message, namely, "Our relationship is more important than this mere trifle."

Never give four of anything. The word for the number four in Japanese is *shi*, also associated with the word for death.

The value of a gift befits the status of the recipient. Never give the same gift to two or more Japanese of unequal rank. Also, unlike in the West, a highly expensive gift is not in any sense considered a bribe.

Gifts are usually exchanged at the end of a visit. Avoid handing over your gift early in the relationship or at any conspicuous moment.

Try not to get caught empty-handed. Wise travelers to Japan automatically carry an assortment of gifts with them just in case. Similarly, experienced companies in the U.S. that may receive Japanese visitors stock a supply of gifts to be drawn from on a moment's notice.

Expect — and respect — reciprocity. You can be certain that if you present a gift, you will soon receive one in return.

Cash handouts should be avoided. Also, avoid gifts with blatant reproductions of your company name or logo. Exceptions to this might be T-shirts or golf caps, which might be classified as souvenirs rather than gifts.

Above all, remember that in Japan gifts are expressions of relationships. The proper gift if considered a true reflection of one's feelings. In Japan gifts come from the heart, not from the wallet or from some obligatory year-end list. In Japan friendship, gratitude, and respect are vital ingredients in business and social relationships.

Finally, in Japan style is just as important as substance. This is true in gift giving and in about all aspects of culture there. Stated still another way: form is just as important as fact.

Japan — What to Give?

Heading this list would be the words "Whatever is difficult to obtain in Japan." Currently, that would include such things as high-grade cuts of beef, fresh fruit, and gourmet foods — in other words, quality foodstuffs not readily available in a country with precious little agrarian space.

The Japanese also prize aged brandy, Scotch and bourbon whiskey, and fine wines. If you choose such spirits, make certain they are top-drawer selections.

Next on the shopping list come products bearing prestigious brand or store names: Tiffany, Steuben, Cartier, Neiman-Marcus, Saks Fifth Avenue, Brooks Brothers, Nordstrom, and the like.

In a separate category come gifts that suggest you have been observant and sensitive toward the recipient's personal interests and tastes. For example, if in some unobtrusive manner you have learned that your Japanese acquaintance collects stamps, crystal figures, coins, or old maps, or has an interest in aviation, antique cars, baseball, or any of a hundred different subjects, this information can provide a bonanza for finding a successful gift.

However, an added note: make certain that whatever you choose is of assured quality and value.

In Japan such careful attention to detail is not only appreciated but noticed and remembered by the recipient. For example, if you happen to know that a pen is a prized personal possession in Japan because it is a symbol of knowledge, pat yourself on the back. But if you also happen to know that because of Japan's distinctive written language *fine pen points* are preferred, then you deserve applause as well.

> *A Case Study:* In this gift category that we have labeled "thoughtfulness" is this charming story. When Ian Kerr of Greenwich, CT learned that a Japanese husband, wife and children had moved into his neighborhood, the Kerr family decided they would like to offer a gesture of welcome. Wisely, the Kerrs preceded their gesture with some research. Learning that on the Japanese calendar a special day honoring children was fast approaching, the Kerr family purchased some typical American toys and, on date of the holiday, presented them to the Japanese family. The toys were merely the tokens. The true gift was the act of researching and respecting a Japanese tradition.

Perhaps at the most modest level of gift giving is the simple souvenir photograph. The Japanese are stereotyped for constantly squinting through camera viewfinders, and they do indeed love to take commemorative photos of almost every gathering. If you are pictured in the group, expect to receive a courtesy copy, and be certain to reciprocate if *you* are the one peering through the lens.

Lastly, avoid sending red Christmas cards to anyone in Japan, since funeral notices there are customarily printed in red.

Later in this chapter you will find a separate list of additional, all-purpose gift suggestions.

Hong Kong

While the Christian tradition of Christmas is celebrated in Hong Kong, the more important gift-giving period there comes at Chinese New Year. Since the Chinese observe a lunar calendar, this may fall at various dates between January 21st and February 19th.

At Chinese New Year the most popular gift among Hong Kongese is a packet of money. The packets traditionally are printed a bright red, often with gold Chinese characters on them.

As for business gift giving in Hong Kong, the British residents are very reserved and unaccustomed to giving or receiving gifts from other Occidentals. Among the Chinese population, however, business gift giving is common and indeed can be extravagant by Western standards. Again, Westerners may be embarrassed by the obvious high cost of a gift received from business associates in Hong Kong and find it difficult to reciprocate. The only recourse is to show special consideration throughout the relationship. This would include such things as offering to provide special favors: helping to obtain theater tickets during visits to the U.S., offering to ship excess baggage back to Hong Kong, assembling information on colleges for the child of an associate, and so on.

With the takeover of Hong Kong by the Chinese in 1997, it is likely that gift-giving practices will be modified to reflect those of the so-called mainland Chinese. It may be helpful to now examine the customs there.

People's Republic of China

Historically, as in many Asian countries whose histories featured feudal hierarchies where currying favor was a way of life, gift giving in China was once a high art form. Then, in 1949, communism came along and made it unlawful to offer gifts to government officials. Now, as communism is relaxing its grip on the people, it is difficult to clearly set down rules and suggestions.

There are, however, a few commonsense guidelines to ease the way.

- One refuge is to present a "group" gift, meaning that your group or company or delegation is offering this token of friendship to the office or department or ministry involved, rather than to an individual person.

- Another recourse is to have your company name appear on the gift so that it is clearly seen as a form of advertising rather than a gift for purely personal gain.

- Another recommendation, especially for anyone associated with the government, is to avoid giving any highly expensive gifts. Once again, a pen happens to be a good choice. The reason is surprisingly simple: The Chinese language consists of ideographs, or "pictures," and therefore it cannot be reduced to fit on an ordinary typewriter keyboard. Consequently, in this land of few typewriters, a quality pen made in the West becomes a valued personal tool.

One idiosyncrasy about gift giving and receiving in China that's important to know: It is proper etiquette to *refuse* the offer of a gift or even a second portion of food or drink. In fact, the Chinese may politely refuse more than once. However, the expectation is that the giver will persist and thus acceptance eventually will follow.

Another piece of etiquette is that, as in Japan, gifts are presented *with two hands*.

As communism becomes more permissive, recent Western visitors are finding that some Chinese are reverting to historical custom and not only accepting but expecting gifts and other favors. An example of this changing ethic is found in the clock. Among the older generation it is considered improper to present a clock as a gift, since the word "clock" in Chinese also carries a morbid, funereal connotation. However, a South Carolina businessman recently found that this has become passé among the younger generation. "In fact, " the businessman reported, "my Chinese customer told me, 'Only old folks believe in that stuff,' and then he specifically *asked* me to bring him one of our fancy digital wall clocks on my next trip."

One long-standing custom is still part of the Chinese "gift-giving" landscape: the banquet or dinner. The warm tradition of a banquet is welcomed and provides an opportunity to salute your Chinese business acquaintances and to get to know them better.

Some remaining gift-giving taboos in China are:

- White, blue, or black gifts are associated with funerals, whereas red, pink, and yellow are "joyful" colors. Yet don't use red ink, because a message written in red implies the severing of a relationship.
- Similarly straw sandals are associated with funerals and therefore considered bad luck.
- Sharp objects — knives, scissors, letter openers — symbolize the cutting off of a friendship.
- Handkerchiefs are a sign of sadness.
- One obscure taboo was encountered by an American agriculturalist, Steve Renk, when he visited northern China. He carried with him green baseball caps bearing his company logo and passed them out to helpful Chinese. . . until he noticed none of the recipients would wear the hats. He later learned that in that part of China, any man wearing a green cap was advertising his daughter for purposes of romance.

On the "good luck" side, there is a saying in Chinese that happiness is "born a twin." That means that two of anything brings good luck; therefore look for gifts that come in pairs. Single items and odd numbers are a sign of separation, loneliness, and death.

In summary, while it is still wise to show restraint when dealing with government officials, change is occurring in China and gift-giving customs appear to be moving slowly back to former practices. That being the case, it is important to take care when selecting a gift.

Taiwan

When it comes to social customs, the rules in Taiwan are an amalgam of those found in the countries surrounding it. Therefore, while gift giving is common, appreciated, and carries many of the intangibles found in Japan, it is less structured and ritualistic than in Japan.

Americans visiting Taiwan, especially the multitude who go there on buying missions, can be embarrassed by the expensive gifts thrust on them by well-meaning associates. For this reason it is wise to have a clear company policy on what an employee can and cannot receive and to carry along an assortment of gifts for reciprocation.

High-quality brand names from top-drawer stores are always appreciated in Taiwan, as is the gift of thoughtfulness. For example, when New Yorker Paul Culp noted that the wife of his Taiwanese business associate offered him a special brand of toffee, he asked where she had obtained it. The woman said, "In the U.S. It's difficult to purchase here in Taiwan." Bingo! Signals flashed in Culp's mind. He later tracked down the source of the toffee in the U.S., and for years thereafter endeared himself to the woman by periodically sending large boxes of the sweets.

One important piece of advice regarding gift giving in Taiwan is to make sure your gift selection comes from high-grade, indigenous sources in America. Taiwan supplied the U.S. with hundreds of millions of dollars of all types of products. As a result, it's entirely possible to inadvertently select a gift in an American store that was made in Taiwan.

Thailand

When visiting a home in Thailand, take flowers or a box of candy or cookies from the local market. The value is not important; it is the thought and the act that count.

It is the tradition in Thailand to wrap gifts beautifully with colorful ribbons, and while the custom has long been to set the gift aside to be opened later, this is not as rigid today. If you are invited to open a gift, avoid ripping open the beautiful wrapping, as this is considered rude.

The Thais love bright colors, so whatever type of gift you may choose, don't be afraid to select strong hues.

Among businesspeople the exchange of relatively modest gifts is common and permitted, especially if presented with the idea that "this is just a token memento of our visit."

Korea

Not surprisingly, gift giving in Korea is very important and, in many ways, similar to the practices of its neighbor Japan.

Generosity is considered a valued personal trait, and it is important to display this with both friends and acquaintances. This not only applies to gifts but to offering extra portions of food and drink.

Among themselves, Koreans exchange gifts on New Year's Day, the Lunar New Year's Day, *Chusok* (the Thanksgiving Day of Korea), and Christmas. Birthdays, graduations, and weddings are also traditional times for presenting gifts.

If visiting someone's home, take along fruit, flowers, cakes, or alcohol.

First and Sixtieth birthdays are extra-special events in Korea, and call for gifts. Money is the traditional gift for weddings, a funeral, or the Sixtieth birthday. Just tuck the cash into an envelope.

Business gifts are exchanged more often and more freely than in the West, but bear in mind that these are expressions of gratitude and considered as symbols rather than as a mere tangible *quid pro quo*.

When handing over a gift, Koreans will belittle the gift, saying, "This is really nothing." For the receiver it is good form to show slight reluctance and hesitation before accepting.

In Korea it is downright impolite to open a gift in the presence of the giver. There's a chance they have read that Westerners do that, however, so if they continue to insist, unwrap it, but with a show of self-restraint.

Once a gift is offered, it should not be refused...unless it smells of an outright bribe. In this case you can always explain that your "company policy" does not permit you to accept such gifts (which, coincidentally, is often the case among U.S. corporations.)

Business gifts in Latin America should not be excessive.

Lastly, don't expect to receive a thank-you note; it is not the custom in Korea.

Singapore and Malaysia

This area is a toughie. The reason is that here you'll find four distinct cultures: Chinese, Malay, Indian, and, in Singapore, British. The first requirement therefore is to determine the nationality of your intended recipient.

For those in the **Chinese** community, reread the suggestions for Hong Kong and Taiwan. In addition, if you are invited to a Chinese home, it is not necessary or expected to bring a gift on the first visit, because that may suggest you are trying to bribe your way into a friendship. On second and third visits, however, bring along some fruit, sweets, or cakes, perhaps adding that "the sweets are for the children." Whatever you select, bring an *even* number, which is a sign of happiness and good luck.

Other customs among the Chinese: The recipient will act very reluctant, so you might say, "I would be happy if you accepted." Don't expect gifts to be opened immediately. Gifts of food are always appreciated. Flowers are not customarily used as gifts.

Among the **Malay** community, here is what you should know.

- Malays accept gifts with pleasure and will often reciprocate.

- Gifts are not opened at the time they are received.

- Muslim rules usually apply: No alcohol. No pork. No personal items (like underwear) as gifts. No knives. No images of dogs or scantily clad women (even a picture of the *Venus de Milo* may be found objectionable).

- Give gifts with the right hand only.

- If invited to a Malay home, try to bring small, "bread-and-butter" gifts for the family. Present the gifts on departing, not when arriving. Good gifts are perfumes and colognes for a hostess, toys for children, and fine cotton shirts (with collars) for men.

In the **Indian** sectors of Malaysia, some of the rules are the same, yet a number are quite different.

- Colors to avoid are white and black. Red, yellow, green, and all bright colors signify happiness.

- When presenting gifts of money, odd numbers are preferred and considered luckier.

- It is impolite to open a gift immediately on receiving it.

- Westerners visiting an Indian home might bring a bowl of fruit, a serving dish filled with sweets, or some attractive *sari* material.

- Among flowers, don't ever give frangipani, a local flower associated with death and funerals.

- Offer a gift with the right hand, and avoid giving cigarettes or alcohol unless you are certain the recipient uses them.

The Middle East

When then President Carter and his wife visited Egypt in 1978, they asked to view a camel market in Cairo. Camel trader Abdel-Wahab Waguih was so honored he not only gave the Carters a tour but also presented them with two silver daggers, several Sudanese camel whips, and a six-year-old camel with a pink ribbon tied around its neck. Waguih also wanted to further honor his guests by slaughtering a sheep at the Carters' feet, a traditional Muslim act of welcome. "But the American Embassy people told me not to, " Waguih said.

What the camel trader was doing was typical of the effusive hospitality and generosity shown in many parts of the Middle East. Within the Arab psyche are these tenets: good manners are an essential ingredient in a person's character, and generosity to guests is essential to a good reputation.

So it should come as no surprise that in the Middle East gift giving is an elevated custom in both personal and business relationships. With that in mind, be careful about admiring a painting, tea server, or any such object at hand, because you just might be the recipient of it . . . right on the spot.

Your Arab colleague will probably initiate the gifting process and, if not at that moment then at the next possible occasion, you should be prepared to reciprocate in kind. That means to reciprocate in elaborateness and cost, if possible. For most Westerners this poses the classic "horns of a dilemma": Staring at you on one horn are U.S. tax and corporate rules, and attached to the other horn is the need to avoid embarrassment and respect the customs of others.

How does the American businessperson, caught in the middle, cope with such a conundrum? One solution is to explain

A banquet is a very acceptable gift in China.
But, be sure you arrange for the correct strata of banquet.

to your desk-bound American compatriots that the firm's very reputation is at stake and thus exceptions are justified, even if this means swallowing any additional after-tax expense. The other recourse is to reciprocate in less tangible ways: assisting your Arab's children who may be attending college in the U.S., helping to arrange for special medical care or treatment in the States for a member of the Arab's family, providing special treatment at hotels whenever the Arab visits here, speeding up a special shipment your customer has ordered, and so on. You get the idea.

In the category of gift taboos, remember the obvious one — never present a Muslim with an alcoholic beverage, since the Islamic faith prohibits the drinking of alcohol. A second wrong move would be to bring gifts for the wife of your Arab colleague — *unless* you have come to know the entire family extremely well. Also, bear in mind that some Arab countries are more conservative than others in following the rules of Islam. Saudi Arabia, for example, is probably the most conservative, while countries like Egypt and Jordan tend to be more liberal.

As for your choice of gifts, make certain they are always of the highest quality, and don't be afraid to flaunt brand names in support of your choice. Silver, porcelain, crystal, fine linens (although handkerchiefs are associated with tears and parting), cashmere, precious and semiprecious stones — any of these would be appropriate choices. Incidentally, when choosing gold objects, keep in mind that Arabs seem to prefer the darker shades of gold, whereas Americans favor the so-called "champagne" hues. Your jeweler can quickly show you the different shadings, from "orange gold" to "white gold."

Fine leather is also appreciated, but avoid pigskin, since pigs are considered scavengers and therefore are shunned within the Muslim diet.

Artwork is always chancy as a gift because of wide diversity in personal tastes, but it is especially so in the Middle East, where showing any exposed parts of the female body is offensive to Muslim teachings.

Speaking of offenses, be very wary of presenting any gift involving Islam's holy book, the Koran, since the teachings of Muhammad are revered and require the utmost respect. At religious holiday times, notably Ramadan (the ninth month in the Islamic calendar), you might be able to locate preprinted greeting cards with authorized excerpts from the Koran. Check with your nearest Saudi Arabian consulate for where these cards might be obtained.

Finally, remember that thoughtfulness is always an appreciated element in a gift. One enterprising Australian businessman devised a unique gift for his Muslim business associate. He learned that devout Muslims must pray five times daily, and that they are required to face Mecca, Islam's holy city, while doing so. Knowing that it is easy to become confused about directions when traveling outside one's own country, the Australian presented his Muslim friend with a sterling silver compass in a beautiful wooden carrying case.

Latin America

Unlike in the Orient and much of the Middle East, gift giving in Latin America is not an elaborate requirement or a formal procedure. Nonetheless, it is important to remember that Latins view business relations as personal relations, and therefore gestures that exhibit kindness, thoughtfulness, and generosity are much appreciated and noted.

For this region of the world, here are some all-purpose suggestions to bear in mind.

- Don't worry about bringing gifts on your first business visit. If you're invited to someone's home, however, first visit or not, don't go empty-handed (see below for suitable hospitality gifts).

- As for categories of gifts, once again a gift of "thoughtfulness" is the best of all choices. This means carefully discerning the likes, tastes, and special interests of your host or business associate and then, on your second visit, demonstrating that awareness.

  Examples:

  If he is a cigar smoker, select the finest cigar tool from America (snipper, puncturer, box opener) you can find.

  If your hostess happens to mention her favorite perfume, bring her a *large* bottle when next you meet.

  If baseball happens to be a passion with your Latin colleague, present him with a valuable piece of baseball memorabilia from the U.S.

  If deep-sea fishing is a favorite sport, take your Latin guests on a *quality* fishing expedition.

If your Latin associates dote over their children, bring the latest electronic toy from the U.S. market. Spare no expense, and double-check that the same item is not already available in their country.

If you discover some favor you can do back in the U.S., kindnesses such as the following will be much appreciated and remembered: assisting a family member in a U.S. college, helping to arrange for medical assistance in the U.S., sending a hard-to-get video or audio cassette release, providing a desired magazine subscription, and so on.

- For more modest occasions, such as being invited to someone's home in Latin America, it is appropriate to bring a fine bottle of liquor or wine or a large box of fancy chocolates. Ask the concierge at your hotel for advice on the specific selection to assure a high-quality choice. Flowers are also appropriate, but certain colors carry unpleasant symbolism in parts of Latin America. For example, in Guatemala white flowers are associated with funerals, in Mexico and Brazil purple flowers have the same connotation and in Chile yellow flowers signify contempt. Therefore, when sending or bringing flowers, check with a local source in advance to make sure you are not sending an unwanted message.

- Bear in mind that some of the world's finest leathers come from South America, specifically, Argentina, Uruguay, and Brazil, so it might be wise to avoid leather gifts unless they are of the highest quality and come with tippy-top brand names.

Australia

Businesspeople rarely exchange elaborate or expensive gifts in Australia. Therefore, when visiting there or when hosting Australians, exchanging such gifts is not expected.

Modest gifts, such as a business diary, a paperweight, or a coffee mug might be presented as a memento of a visit or business meeting. At a sales conclave or trade show, T-shirts, ties, baseball caps, or a pin may be appropriate mementos.

Anything more than these types of gifts could cause embarrassment in a society known for its friendly informality and lack of pretentiousness.

The United Kingdom
(England, Wales, Scotland, Northern Ireland)

Business gift giving in the U.K. reflects the pattern in the U.S., but perhaps with even more restraint. There is a thriving advertising specialty, premium, and service awards industry in the U.K. This means gifts are often marked with company names, used as merchandising incentives, or used for recognition events.

According to one respected guide on etiquette in England, *Debrett's Etiquette & Modern Manners* (Headline, London, 1981), "When going to stay at a very grand house, it is not correct to take a gift. Almost everywhere else it is nice to do so but not absolutely necessary and the nature of the gift depends very much on the circumstances." Otherwise, when going to a country cottage or a person's residence, it would be thoughtful to inquire if you might bring a bottle of wine but, as Debrett cautions,"[Gifts] are better sent after the visit, when you have had a chance to establish your hosts' interests."

Debrett also cautions that bringing a book, flowers, or wine to a dinner party might inconvenience the hostess, who must take time to admire the book, arrange the flowers, or quickly replace the wine already selected.

Debrett, the protocol bible of England, doesn't provide any advice at all on the subject of business gift-giving, dismissing the practice as unimportant.

Austria

Many of the same rules that apply in Germany (see below) also apply in Austria: when invited to a home, bring an odd number of flowers but not red roses, unwrap them, and so on. Also, in Austria avoid red carnations, since they are usually reserved for May Day.

Belgium

As in the adjacent areas of Northern and Central Europe, business gift giving is very low-key and usually takes the form of day-to-day, mundane-type gifts: diaries or appointment books, a business-related or topical book from your country, products with your company logo discreetly placed on them, and so on. If you do wish to honor someone with a special gift, however, check the list of additional suggestions at the end of this chapter.

Eastern European countries

All the countries in this region are starved for Western consumer goods. This means everything from blue jeans to audiocassettes and from quality pens to the latest electronic products. If you choose the latter, however, because of differing electrical power strengths it's best to select products that operate on batteries.

Just about anything you care to pack in your suitcase probably will be gratefully received by business contacts or, for that matter, anyone who has been of assistance and whom you wish to recognize with a "thank-you" gift. Be careful, however, about bringing large quantities of any type of gift lest you generate suspicion that you are aiming to trade on the black market.

According to *Robert T. Moran's Cultural Guide to Doing Business in Europe* (Butterworth-Heinemann, Oxford, England, 1992), the most popular medium of exchange in Eastern Europe is a bottle of vodka, especially a good brand name vodka, which is often difficult to obtain there. Women appreciate receiving cosmetics, because they also are scarce in almost all Eastern European countries. When yellow flowers are given, it is a sign of grieving or separation. When invited to a home, it is proper social etiquette to bring a bottle of liquor or wine, flowers, or chocolates, but nothing too expensive.

France

There are few rules for gift-giving protocol in France, mainly because the exchange of gifts between business associates is not common or expected. Businesses may present fairly modest products marked discreetly with the company name to favored customers but, as with many customs in France, conservatism rules.

Socially, when invited to dinner it might be appropriate to express your appreciation by sending flowers to the hostess on the following day, but avoid red roses and chrysanthemums, because the former suggest romance and the latter death.

Germany

Business gift giving is fairly restrained in Germany, but businesses will pass out gift products for purposes of advertising, promotion, incentives, and employee recognition. Also, at Christmas some retail stores might give special calendars or diaries to their regular customers.

Social gift giving is popular and well established in Germany and has certain do's and don'ts that are worth noting.

• Modest gifts might be given as tokens of friendship. For example, in Germany you can purchase miniature boxes containing one chocolate with a miniature gift card attached.

• When visiting a German home, gifts that reflect your home country are popular, and you might want to bring small gifts for the children of the family you are visiting.

• Gifts are customarily wrapped and many Germans spend considerable time designing elegant wrappings. Most shops and large stores offer gift-wrapping services, too.

• Flowers are often taken to a hostess of a dinner party at her home, but there are three taboos to remember: 1) red roses signify a romantic interest, 2) an even number of flowers signifies bad luck, as does the number thirteen, and 3) always unwrap the flowers before presenting them.

Greece

Rather than outright gifts, an evening's entertainment is probably the most common form of showing appreciation in Greece. According to Moran, if you do present a gift, avoid personal items, such as ties, shirts, and cuff links. Instead, steer toward such things as coffee-table books, desk sets, and table lighters. If you are invited to a Greek home, flowers or a cake for the hostess are an appropriate gift.

Italy

Business gift giving follows the pattern described in the U.K. and Germany; in other words, it is not a requirement and it does not bear strong protocols.

Socially, when you are invited to a person's home for dinner, it might be nice to bring flowers or a box of chocolates for your hostess, although it is just as considerate to have the flowers sent the next day.

As in much of Europe, red roses suggest "romance, secrecy, and passion," while yellow roses can signify "jealousy." Again, flowers should be sent in odd numbers, but avoid the number thirteen. And in Italy *never* send chrysanthemums, since they belong only on coffins and graves.

Scandinavia

Elaborate or expensive business gifts are neither necessary nor expected in the Scandinavian countries (Denmark, Norway, and Sweden) or in Finland. However, a gesture that is always appreciated is to buy a good bottle of whiskey or cognac at the duty free shops at your embarkation airport and then present it to anyone who does you a favor, such as meeting you at the airport and driving you to your hotel.

The presentation of token gifts — such as modestly priced products with your company name imprinted on them — is common and will not cause embarrassment, but extravagant gifts will be suspect and perhaps even unwelcome.

When invited to someone's home for dinner, a bouquet of flowers or a box of fine chocolates is appropriate.

Russia

The Russian people are enthusiastic gift givers, very spontaneous, and present giving is a part of their life. In addition, it is well known that they have lacked many of the daily products Westerners take for granted. As a result, when visiting Russia it would be wise to pack an assortment of Western consumer goods to use as gifts. The one commodity perhaps in greatest demand is cigarettes. But just about any item you bring can be used on the local barter market to obtain other desired items. So the list of possible gifts is endless.

Here are some thought-starters: T-shirts, audiocassettes of pop music, baseball caps, brand name pens, gourmet food, just about any electronic item, and duty free liquor.

More modest gifts include pictures of your home city or state, small items of clothing, good soap, and books in English or French.

For more ambitious gifts travelers take blue jeans, professional sports team sweatshirts and jackets, sports footwear, and even laptop computers. Be careful about taking large quantities of any of these, however, because you will be suspected of trading on the black market.

Of course, it will be difficult for your hosts or business associates in Russia to reciprocate, but your gift will be appreciated to the fullest by the receiver.

Other Countries

For countries not mentioned above, you can assume that business gift giving is neither required nor filled with frightful idiosyncrasies. For those countries keep these suggestions in mind:

When invited to a private home for dinner, consider bringing a bottle of good spirits (something *not* available locally, if possible), expensive chocolates, or flowers.

In the case of flowers, check with local sources to assure that your choice has no special local symbolism; also, consider the alternative of sending the flowers the next day along with a thank-you note.

Let's say that you have not brought along any gifts and that you feel indebted to people either for favors they have performed or entertainment they have provided. In these cases it may be appropriate to host a dinner for them at a quality local restaurant. When you issue the invitation, make certain your business friends understand that you wish to serve as the host. Tell them the time and place, emphasize that you would like them to be your guests, and then also make arrangements with the maître d'hôtel to pay for the evening in advance or separately.

Another way to make your gift memorable is to have it carry a secondary message.

Example: A crystal or porcelain replica of an eagle is a nice gift in itself, but it can carry with it a patriotic American message, or it can suggest achievement, such as "flying to new heights" or "acting with precise vision."

Another example: A leather briefcase is a perfectly fine gift, but one that bears barbed wire scars carries a vision of the American Western cowboy, corrals, and roundups.

A third example: A set of commemorative coins is another excellent gift, but if they also happen to represent a date or place that is significant between the presenter and the recipient, the gift will be remembered longer.

Some Specific Gift Suggestions

Each of us would like to be *creative* enough to find that truly "perfect" gift. But that is indeed a tough assignment. A Chicago advertising executive once described the creative process thusly: "Let's say my assignment is to create an advertising idea for selling a piano. If I were to be placed in a bare room with just a typewriter and a blank sheet of paper and try to create a winning collection of ideas, I would most likely fail. However, if I could paper the walls of that same room with examples of past ad campaigns for pianos, and with campaigns from other piano makers, and with examples of successful advertising ideas for other musical products . . . the odds are much better that I could be creative. I wouldn't necessarily copy or imitate any single idea on the walls around me, but they would surely spark some new twist that would provide just the right answer."

Like that advertising executive, you may not necessarily find that "perfect" gift suggestion in what follows, but if you imagine this list as pasted on the bare walls of your mind, the "right answer" might just suddenly materialize.

We start with a collection of ideas for the international visitor:

- Anything having to do with the American West: genuine arrowheads, Native American jewelry, picture books of the Old West, a pair of cowboy boots, and so on.

- Unique products from your state or region: Vermont maple syrup, Wisconsin cheeses, saltwater taffy, cranberry relish, products made by Quakers or the Amish, or Moravian cookies from South Carolina.

- Products that represent your city or state: woods or stones indigenous to your area, picture or history books, medallions, or carvings. Travel writer Jane Merrill Filstrup reports that the Japanese seem to enjoy Eskimo carvings, the French like our quilting and appliqué work, and many Germans covet our Western hats, accessories, and clothes.

- Something that you have made with your own hands, such as jewelry, needlepoint, preserves, or candy.

- Almost anything connected with Disney, Walt Disney World, or Disneyland.

- *Avoid* giving fitness-related gifts (e.g., exercise equipment) lest you imply the receiver needs physical improvement.

- A book of Norman Rockwell reproductions or Ansel Adams photographs.

- A Paul Revere bowl (both historic and useful).

- Musical tapes or compact discs, if you know the recipient's tastes.

- Subscriptions to American magazines, especially *National Geographic*.

- And finally, after thirteen-year-old Rikke Olsen of Denmark spent six weeks in the U.S., she returned home happily laden with stacks of Oreo cookies, jars of crunchy peanut butter, two novelty telephones, and scads of packets of bubble gum.

Gift suggestions for the frequent traveler:

- One *New York Times* writer claims the best travel gift she ever got was a set of compact, high-quality, folding binoculars.

- Also high on her list was a travel alarm clock with numbers visible enough for a dark hotel room. (Business executive John Tries tells why he, too, prefers carrying his own alarm clock. Checking into a hotel in France, he examined the clock provided by the hotel and worried it wasn't operating properly. When he complained to the concierge, the Frenchman shrugged off Tries' objections with this solution: "If in the morning it doesn't work . . . call me.")

- Along with an alarm clock, veteran travelers always pack a small, collapsible, nylon carryall bag inside their regular suitcase. It becomes invaluable if you're the kind that seems to return home with more clothes or souvenirs than you departed with.

- An inflatable neck pillow.

- A small, high-quality flashlight. If you've ever experienced a power failure at night in an unfamiliar hotel, you'll know firsthand the value of one of these.

- A collapsible umbrella, or a light poncho that folds into a magazine-thin packet.

- A lightweight, one-size-fits-all, foldable travel bathrobe. Also, good leather travel slippers.

- A Swiss army knife, especially one equipped with a bottle and can opener.

- Enroll your guest (or client, or customer) in one of the airline VIP clubs. Select an airline that serves his or her country as well as yours.

- A portable audiocassette player with earphones.

- A portable, electric, dual voltage clothes steamer to remove those inevitable wrinkles from suits and dresses.

- A small, portable water purifier (for the traveler who is known to venture into distant corners of the map.)

- A compact, battery-powered AM/FM receiver, with equally portable earphones, along with instructions on how to tune in the Voice of America and the BBC World Service.

- A quality security pouch for carrying passport and money. These come in many shapes and styles, from conventional money belts to holders that can be draped around the neck or suspended inside a skirt or trousers on a belt at the waist, to the kind that are strapped around the ankle.

- Two decks of playing cards (of the highest quality, of course). These may just save the day for the traveler confronted by airline delays or cancellations.

- In any book partly published by The Parker Pen Company, it's appropriate to include a word about why *pens* are good business gifts. The company founder, George S. Parker, was fond of saying, "Our pens write in any language." That was not just hubris, either. Today Parker pens are known and respected in every country in the world. Ironically, in much of Europe and Asia, Parker is actually better known than in the U.S. In fact, in some regions of the world, it is reported that only Parker pen *caps* are carried in shirt or coat pockets, the reason being that the person is actually illiterate but "wears" the pen cap to imply that he or she is, in fact literate, and also has had the means to purchase a Parker pen.

Pens make good business gifts for several reasons:

- They are small in size, and you can pack as many as a dozen quite easily inside any suitcase.

- If you pack an assortment (some plastic, some stainless, some silver, some gold), you'll probably have a gift suitable for everyone from the concierge to the chairman of the board.

- Parker is known and respected around the world for quality and luxury; also, its products probably cost more outside the U.S., so the receiver knows he or she is the beneficiary of true value.

- Your company logo can be easily marked on or affixed to the pen. Or you can have the recipient's name or initials engraved on barrels or caps.

- Finally, a pen is a safe gift. There are absolutely no taboos associated with pens (in fact, in Thailand at one time the word for "pen" was "Parker."

Tipping: A Gift Or A Bribe?

Some unknown English innkeeper apparently started it all. Near the door of his inn, he placed a brassbound box to receive coins from customers. The box was labeled To Insure Promptitude.

That very likely gave birth to the modern-day word "tip," taken from the first letters of those Old English words. But is a tip a bribe or a gift? The answer is not always clear.

The French call a tip *pourboire*, the literal translation meaning "for a drink" or implying "have a drink on me as thanks for your service." In German, it is *trinkgeld*, a "drink gift." In Spanish, a tip is a *propina*.

The Spanish *propina* should not be confused with the Spanish word for "bribe," which is *mordida*, meaning, literally, "small bite." The editor of this text was once asked to carry a package from a U.S. company to its Mexican subsidiary. Worried that Mexican customs officials might hassle the bearer, the senders kiddingly affixed a note to the parcel that said, "Watch out for the *mordida*!" Not knowing either the word or the practice, the editor waltzed right through the customs counters with the note still stuck on top, wondering about all the fishy looks.

Before recounting tipping practices around the world, let's have a vocabulary lesson.

In **many countries** the word "tip" is not used; instead it is called a "gratuity."

In **Turkey, Egypt, India, and certain other Eastern countries,** *baksheesh* is a gratuity or gift of alms. But it has also come to mean "a kickback."

In **Brazil,** an important word to know *jeito*, which basically means, "You do a favor for me, and I'll do a favor for you." Money rarely changes hands.

In various parts of **Africa,** *dash* is the word for a monetary gift that is customary and expected for getting anything from a visa to a favored airplane seat.

In **Southeast Asia,** *kumshaw* is the word for a bribe.

In the **U.S.,** "grease" is another term for "facilitating payments." This refers to perfectly legal payments of modest sums to foreign officials for speedy performance of their normal duties.

Now let's take a satellitelike spin around the globe and peer down at tipping practices in selected countries.

In **Canada** and the **United States**, 15 percent is the customary tip for a dinner bill, more if the service was exceptional. For taxis, 10 percent is appropriate. One suggestion: In Canada, tip with local money rather than U.S. bills or coins.

In **Mexico,** tipping is a large chunk of working life. Wages there are often so low that service workers depend heavily on gratuities. You'll observe many open palms. Even when you park a car on the street, young *watchacaros* will appear and promise to "watch your car."

In **Western Europe,** as a general rule an additional charge ranging anywhere from 10 to 20 percent is *automatically* added to your hotel and dining bills. For travelers unaccustomed to this, *it is recommended that each and every time you check into a hotel or begin to pay a dinner check, you ask, "Is service included?"* For other, special services, a separate small payment can be added.

Note: Major European cities where this is customary include Amsterdam, Brussels, Copenhagen, Geneva, Helsinki, Moscow, Oslo, Paris, Stockholm, and Zurich.

In **Germany** you'll encounter a tipping peculiarity: if and when the 15 percent gratuity is automatically added to your dinner tab, and if you pay in cash, always leave the loose coins in the tray when you receive your change.

In **Japan** and **Singapore**, tips are usually included in the food bill. Elsewhere in the Far East, be sure to ask before paying.

Taxis present a different set of rules. Tips are usually included in the fare in cosmopolitan cities like Amsterdam, Athens, Bangkok, Brussels, Copenhagen, Geneva, Helsinki, Moscow, Oslo, Singapore, Tokyo, and Zurich. In other large cities, a tip of 5 to 10 percent is appropriate.

In some **Arab** nations, taxi drivers theoretically don't take tips, but as *Business Week* magazine reports, "[If you don't tip] your fare may mysteriously double at the end of your ride. Always agree on fares before climbing into an unmetered taxi."

In three places in the world — **the People's Republic of China, Iceland** and **Tahiti** — *tips are considered inappropriate.*

In **Latin America,** tipping practices and tipping amounts are difficult to catalog. Therefore, the best advice for that region — indeed, good advice for anywhere — is, immediately upon arrival, ask the concierge at your hotel or a local friend for advice on the rules for tipping. All over the world both overtipping and undertipping are viewed as rude and inconsiderate, so the A-L-F "ask a local friend" rule becomes fundamental protocol for the wise traveler.

For further information, see Nancy Star's *The International Guide to Tipping* (Berkley Books, New York, 1988), which contains a country-by-country guide for tipping in every conceivable situation, from fishing boat crews to casino croupiers.

Finally, in 1985 *Fortune* magazine recorded what is probably the granddaddy of all tips: Two limousines drew up to a New Orleans restaurant just as it was about to close, and a party of Kuwaiti oilmen, with bodyguards and wives, disembarked. The maître d'hôtel agreed to stay open. After salads and soft drinks, the bill came to $185. The tip? The customers left $20,000, with instructions to "keep the change."

Now *that*'s what one would call recognizing promptitude.

Ten Final Tips
For Graceful Gift Giving

1. Whenever traveling abroad, it is *always* wise to pack a few small, medium-priced gifts in your suitcase for emergencies. Have them wrapped in unobtrusive, pastel colors, perhaps slipping your business card inside the wrapping.

2. Small, inexpensive gifts (key chains, corporate medallions, inexpensive diaries, cheap pens) are acceptable as casual "leave-behind" tokens, but they should never be considered a substitute for a proper business gift.

3. To minimize any possible embarrassment for the recipient of a business gift, accompany the gift with such words as, "This in not intended as a gift, but merely as a small memento of this visit."

4. When sending gifts to people in other countries, be certain to check on the customs duties that will be applied. In many countries luxury products can carry punishing tariffs, and the end cost to the recipient could be substantial.

5. When choosing a gift to present to an international traveler visiting the U.S., pay special attention to the size and weight of the gift. Bear in mind that your visitor must pack your gift in a suitcase and possibly may have several more stops on the itinerary before returning home. If for some special reason your gift selection is large, heavy, or bulky, it would be courteous to offer to ship the gift to the recipient's home. Once again, inquire about possible restrictions and heavy import duties and prepay those if possible.

6. In many large U.S. cities, it is possible to find "gift consultants" listed in the yellow pages of your phone directory. While many of these may not be expert in international gift giving, they still may be able to suggest novel, locally made products to fit your needs.

7. If you have any misgivings about a gift you are considering, a useful source for information in the U.S. is the cultural attaché at the foreign embassy of the country you plan to visit. It can be worth a phone call to this official or department to assure you are not committing a gaffe. Contact directory assistance for Washington, D.C. (1-202-555-1212) and ask for the telephone number of the appropriate embassy.

8. Gifts with your company logo emblazoned in large letters should be considered as advertising, so use them only if such a piece of promotion would be appropriate.

9. Personalizing your gift is very often a special touch that will be appreciated by the recipient. This could involve anything from etching or printing or engraving the person's full name on the product (or its holder, base, or container) to very subtly placing the person's initials in an inconspicuous but tasteful place.

10. Remember that even though a gift of flowers or wine has been mentioned frequently in this chapter, each has its drawbacks. Handing a hostess a bouquet of flowers might embarrass other guests who have come empty-handed, as well as forcing her to scurry around putting them in a vase and placing them in a visible spot. As for a bottle of wine, one bottle may not be enough for all the invited guests, and furthermore, your hosts may have already selected and stocked a favored wine suited to their menu. Solutions to each of these circumstances: send flowers either before or after the event, and if and when you present the wine, explain, "This is for you to enjoy on some other special occasion."

CHAPTER 4

American Jargon
and
Baffling Idioms

International misunderstandings,
or
Why a German understands a Japanese speaking English, but neither may understand an American

U.S. industry sends forth thousands of emissaries each year, confident that wherever they take their act, their language is sure to be spoken. Too bad so many forget to ask, but will it be *understood*? That blissful indifference has created a modern-day "Tower of Business Babel."

American business is one of the worst offenders in language proliferation. Imagine the confusion of your overseas business contact when on one trip he meets the Personnel Director only to find on the next visit that the same person is now called (as is the growing custom) Director of Human Resources. Same with the fellow in charge of insurance; he is now Director of Risk Management. American business has created *two* types of auditors: internal and external. And if you are still not convinced, try to find someone who calls himself or herself a "salesperson." They are now all "account managers" or "service representatives."

The way the mother tongue trips from our lips these days — tintinnabulating with buzzwords, cusswords, puns, gags, technical and business jargon, sports and military metaphors, show biz zingers, hyperbole, euphemisms, Latinisms, and all the other isms from local to colloquial — is it any wonder that it ends up sounding like Greek to everyone else?

Ambiguity's price can be steep, far costlier than a lost laugh or a dent in the conversational flow. Why should a Saudi purchasing agent buy from an American whose English he finds unfathomable, when the same language as spoken by a French or Japanese salesman comes across loud and clear?

Communications Crisis

A questionnaire on the subject of international communications was completed by 204 corporate executives, business owners, consultants, trainers, bankers, and other movers and shakers with high mileage in overseas trade. *It is clear that America faces a communications crisis that neither Berlitz nor bytes alone can solve.* Fully 80 percent of these business travelers reported difficulties conducting business with foreigners because of the latter's misunderstanding of American English. They also pointed out that the answer lies with us — not with technology. In other words, if the message is not clear, the medium cannot help.

Let's deal first with our sins, then with our salvation as suggested by the tips and cautionary tales from these respondents.

The Seven Deadliest Sins
of International Misunderstanding

Local color

Jargon

Slang

Officialese

Humor

Vocabulary

Grammar

Local Color: From Idioms to Accents

As nervous as a long-tailed cat
in a room full of rocking chairs.

A memorable way to make your point, perhaps — unless your audience has never seen a rocking chair. We tend to take the fixtures of our American culture, from rockers to home runs, for granted. As a result, the word pictures we Americans paint are often seen by others as a jumble of foreign objects.

Flat as a pancake
Safe as Fort Knox
Old as Methuselah
Funny as a rubber crutch

. . . and clear as mud to a citizen of Peru or the Punjab. Even when all the words are familiar, the figure of speech itself can be baffling, even insulting.

Raining cats and dogs
Flying by the seat of your pants
Coming up roses
Don't make waves
Keep a low profile

Most of us do not stop to realize how many of our metaphors come right off the playing field — and not Eton's but the Astrodome's. No matter how avid a golfer or baseball fan your foreign counterpart is, American sports terminology is still likely to leave him out in left field.

Asking for a ballpark figure rarely gets you to first base. Aces, end runs, slam dunks, and playing for all the marbles are not worldwide business maneuvers. One U.S. firm lost a client simply because of the remark, "This is a whole new ball game." The client did not consider the discussion a game. But then, how would you cope with a Spaniard who habitually laced his replies with bullring terms? "Excuse me, señor, but I must do a paso doble to your proposal."

Bonjour, tristesse

Once the tongue of diplomats, courtesans, and other dignitaries, French has, *hélas*, fallen on sad times. For Americans, at least, it is now mere punctuation: *Mon dieu! Zut alors! Entre nous. A chacun son goût* . . . .

It's not that we lack perfectly good English to say the same thing. But there will always be those (or as Miss Piggy would say, "But surely, sweets, not *moi!*") who feel the urge to Frenchify. If this is one of your weaknesses, better not give in to it when on the road. Especially on *la rue*. Lovers of the language (including most educated Europeans, North Africans, and other peoples colonized by the French) hate the way we pronounce it. And nonlovers of the language will neither know nor care what all the *entre nous*es and *son goût*s are about.

Hail, Caesar

One of the oldest languages is also one of the latest to invade the conference room. Not even the mailroom clerks seem able to keep the *per ses*, *ad hocs*, and *quid pro quos* out of their syntax.

A touch of Latin can make a weak-kneed sentence sound more authoritative, perhaps. But unless your field is religion or the law, there are good English equivalents — and good reasons to use them. One, you don't risk the usual misusages and overusages. Two, you don't embarrass the Japanese engineer who spent twenty years mastering English but, unsurprisingly, still does not know an *id est* from an *a priori*. Three, you don't look silly to the English stenographer who was translating *The Aeneid* while the rest of us were sounding out Dr. Seuss.

"Look, Ali, if you folks will play ball with my team, we can split
homerun profits with double play efficiency..."

There are many Latin words embedded in our language that we *cannot* do without. Yet they still have not become anglicized enough to be treated like regular English; for example, media, data, algae, stimulus, curriculum — et cetera. There's no danger they will be misunderstood by others, but big danger they will be misspoken by *us*.

All too few executives appear to be aware that the singular of media is not media — or that the plural of curriculum is not just a matter of adding an *s* — or that data takes a plural verb, not an "is" or a "was." But never mind if you never took Latin 101. Just find someone who did and ask for a crash course in endings. (Total semester time: about ten minutes.)

When in Rome, then, do not necessarily say what the Romans say — or said. Also, do not necessarily say what you say at home. And that goes for the *way* you say it as well.

Ciao to all that

Down-home accents and word variations can be incomprehensible even to someone well versed in standard American English as pronounced by television commentators and language instructors. For instance, a Texas businessman reports that an innocent "y'all" got him into hot water right in his own backyard. When he urged his client from overseas, "Y'all come for another visit," the visitor interpreted it to mean he should return with more people next time.

Still another "y'all" invitation, this one in Jedda, insulted the sheiks it was meant for, because they assumed it included their subordinates.

Beware of drawls and twangs. They may be colorful, but they can make the simplest syllable come out like a trombone note dipped in motor oil ("caay-yunt" for "can't"), while big-city talk often chews words up and spits them out like day-old Bazooka gum ("wadja" for "what did you").

Even after you tame the accent, remember, *not too fast and not too slow*. Fast is hard to grasp and slow is patronizing. "You can actually judge an American's experience in export," claims one corporate officer, "by the rate of his speech."

Repetition doesn't hurt, either. As the old Madison Avenue adage goes, "Tell 'em what you're gonna tell 'em. Tell 'em. Then tell 'em what you told 'em." It sells a lot of cornflakes, and it works on a lot of non-Americans who would rather miss your point than lose face admitting they missed it.

Ordinary Language

The editor of this book traveled with a small group of Americans to the People's Republic of China in 1976. Included in the group was a famous trademark attorney. One evening the Chinese took the two of us aside and said, "We need your advice. One of you has experience in consumer goods, the other in registering trademarks. We wish to sell our sewing machines in America and would like your reaction to the brand name we have chosen."

"What name do you want to use?" asked the Americans.

"We want to call it," said the Chinese with great pride, "the 'Ordinary Sewing Machine.' "

We Americans could not help wincing. To our careful queries into why they had chosen the name "ordinary," the Chinese officials explained, "That is the direct translation from our language. Besides, in our country with our classless society, it is a good term. Why? Is it bad in America?"

"Yes," we answered. Ordinary, we explained, meant "common," and they would do better to call their machine the "Supremo" or the "Premier." This clearly troubled the Chinese, and after a night of contemplation, they returned in the morning with this puzzled rejoinder.

"You remember you said that 'ordinary' was a bad word for a brand name in America because it meant 'common'?"

We remembered.

"How is it, then, that in America you have the Standard Oil Company?"

One piece of advice comes from a lady with a dog-eared passport and a VP on her letterhead. "Speak to the rest of the world," she says, "as if answering a slightly deaf, very rich old auntie who just asked you how much to leave you in her will."

In at least one culture, the Japanese, *silence* is an important aspect of clear communications. Americans abhor silence; those gaps must be filled. But among the Japanese it is common — even expected — to have periods of silence in which the Japanese businessman contemplates what has been said. The Japanese cannot understand why an American dislikes those quiet moments. As one Japanese businessman asked, "Do American businesspeople think and talk at the same time?"

Finally, keep in mind that your English-as-a-second-language business counterpart may take your words quite literally. One midwestern executive sent a cable to his Peruvian manager saying, "Send me factory and office headcount broken down by sex." The reply came, "249 in factory, 30 in office, 3 on sick leave, none broken down by sex — our problem is with alcohol."

Jargon: The tongue without a brain

Why think when you can just talk? Jargon is to communication approximately what painting by numbers is to art. Somebody else works out the logistics, then we take our little kit and dab the colors in the appropriate spaces. An "input" here. A "feedback" there. "Bottom lines" everywhere.

Is there anyone among us who hasn't met the systems analyst who lost the power to say anything but "interface" the year the silicon chip was invented? Too bad for those nice old pensioned-off words that used to do the job — "share," "coordinate," "work together," "common ground"— all forced into early retirement as soon as the upstart grabbed the reins. But wait. Interface's number will soon be up, for it is in jargon's very genes to die a sudden and unmourned death. (Remember when not even a salami was worth a second glance unless it was "state of the art"?)

The trick is to detect the moment when those vital signs begin to falter. Using yesterday's buzzword today ("buzzword" currently being everyone's favorite buzzword) is as fatal a career move as rolling a Hula Hoop to the office.

Words to be wariest of are those with a high-tech heritage, since they keep changing as quickly as the industry that hatches them. On the other hand, terms from such notably low-tech spheres as banking and advertising have been around so long even a Kazakhstani could probably read you. That does not guarantee, however, that the Englishman next to him could, too.

On the same wavelength
Shotgun approach
Overview
Run it up the flagpole
Downtime
Wallpaper the meeting
1OOK (for 100,000)
Sandbag
It will never fly
Dog and pony show
On a roll*

Understanding them depends on how many jet stream Willy Lomans your overseas contacts have encountered. So why not avoid following in Willy's footsteps altogether? Put it as only you can put it. Not only will it sound much more sincere, but searching for your own words crystalizes the whole thought, while clichés allow the sentences to slip off your tongue causing scarcely a blip on your EEG.

Please remember, though, that *all* esoterica is not jargon. Every profession has its own insider language for which there is no legitimate substitute. Even if it is changing every nanosecond, there is nothing trendy or slangy about this kind of terminology. A regional manager in the communications industry cites a few examples he is currently coping with.

Frequency hopping
Spread spectrum
Shake, rattle, roll
SNAPS technology
System architecture

Whether you take your business lexicon as far as Lima, Ohio, or Lima, Peru, never assume even your opposite number there knows what you are talking about. An American representing his company on a swing through Germany tells of breezing through a description of a heat-treating process called pickling. The German interpreter stopped him short and grabbed a dictionary. Nonetheless, the best German equivalent she could offer her *obermeisters* was *gurke*. So instead of "pickling," they got "cucumber."

---

*Not from the hot dog industry but a sporticism meaning running like Herschel Walker through the business world.

A "dog and pony show" is not a dog and pony show.

Coast-speak

A lot of pin-striped jargon may have gone to Harvard Business School, but all the more unbuttoned manifestations of the form took the red-eye in direct from the Coast. (There is only one Coast, incidentally, and it is not the North, South, or East one.)

Cradle of high tech, California has also given us that socio- and psycho-babble into which even the squarest of us lapse when not fiercely vigilant or entirely sober.

Friendships, love affairs, even lifelong loathing no longer exist. Instead, there are "relationships." When somebody says he wants to "share" something with you, he is referring not to his wine or his wife but the story of his life. California, of course, is where long ago someone invited a few friends over to grump about a dull job or a philandering spouse and had the genius to call it consciousness-raising. (A whole new industry was born.) Now any get-together with a serious agenda such as politics, foreplay, or macrobiotic mulching is a workshop. To use such terms outside the privacy of your own hot tub is bad taste. To use them outside the *country* is positively xenophobic.

Yet another California product that travels fast but not well is the verb. Anyone within five Ferrari lengths of Rodeo Drive "takes" a meeting, "does" drugs (or carrot juice or *some*thing), and above all "flows." This last denotes the much envied ability to stay cool even if one's six-figure contract just blew out to Catalina. Whatever you claim on a conference call to L.A. (*never* Los Angeles, of course), let it not be that you are "laid back" or you will hear nothing but clicks on the other end. The phrase of the day is "kicked back," though what it will be by the time this line comes back from the printer, who knows?

General Confusion in Command

"Reentry," "burnout," "abort," "jettison," etc. have all been given new life — and new meaning — by the military. Once a word has been to Mars, not many earthlings will forget its meaning. But what most of us do trip over is that Space-Shuttle-to-Command-Central habit of calling a spade not a spade but a "facility" or "mode" or some other Houstonized nonword that requires half a dozen more before anyone knows what is going on. A facility can, in fact, be anything from the launchpad to the space arm to the head.

Businesspeople have taken to this not *double*talk but *quintuple* talk like astronauts to moon dust. Words become phrases, phrases paragraphs, and your audience paralyzed. Nothing loses a foreign ear faster than a parade of modifiers struggling to do what the subject of the sentence should have done in the first place. In short, call a toilet a toilet — not a "relief facility."

Jargon Lives!

As the updated edition of this book goes to press, American jargon — like some monstrous ooze created by horror writer Stephen King — continues to flow and flow, spilling into every crevice of our language . . . and confusing the hell out of all non-English-speaking people.

Each year brings a new outpouring, often covering last year's stream. For example, the "Valley Girl" lingo of the early 1980s is out. Now playing the "oxymoron game" is in. (Oxymoron — a pair of English words that actually contradict each other. Examples: jumbo shrimp, metal wood (as in golf), fair tax, epic miniseries, guest host, etc.)

The American business world is especially guilty. Five years ago the following list of current in-vogue terms would have been considered meaningless and nonsensical: "laptop" (How can a lap have a top?), "desktop publishing" (That takes a very small printing press), "fax" (Do you mean "fix"?), "read my lips" (Why? I can hear you very clearly), "spin doctor" (Does he specialize in acute dizziness?), and "catastrophic health insurance" (Seems to me in a true catastrophe, I wouldn't need any health insurance.)

Is this American predisposition for creating new terms really a problem in cross-cultural communication? Well, consider the 1988 Summer Olympics in South Korea. A T-shirt design innocently created by NBC television workers created a furor. Inspired perhaps by Michael Jackson, the group had shirts printed with the slang expression "We're Bad" and a drawing of two boxers in the middle of a South Korean flag. The action was intended to spur on the U.S. Olympic boxers. Instead, it created an international incident with the South Koreans. Both the slogan, which was taken literally, and the insensitive use of the Korean flag offended them.

If you're still unconvinced that Americans, and particularly American businesses, spawn an unceasing amount of jargon, imagine an overseas visitor who learned English long ago in

"Change the order. The American says 'scratch the potatoes.'"

some distant classroom coping with this list of contemporary words:

hacker
computer virus
hog heaven
yuppie
gridlock
leveraged buyouts

parenting
number crunching
gifting
condo
power lunch
couch potato

Sharon Richards, coordinator of cross-cultural training for Intel Corporation, Santa Clara, California, compiled an extensive glossary of American business slang to help foreign-speaking employees learn our vexing expressions. "Going to a baseball game," she says, "and just using the terminology of baseball is like speaking an entirely new, remote, and befuddling language to a visitor."

And if you consider our jargonesque nature to be harmless and amusing, just a manifestation of our living language, others take their words and slang more seriously. Take the Germans, for example. According to an account in *Time* magazine, Bavarians who may impulsively call a traffic officer a *damischer Bulle* (stupid bull) can be fined an average of $1,710. If you label the officer a *Raubritter* (robber baron), the levy is $1,140. Calling him a *Depp* (idiot) will cost you $513. And calling him a "smelly boot" (*Stinkstiefel*) may be worth the bargain price of $51.

American jargon is a living, growing, shifting, spawning, creeping, befuddling idiosyncrasy of our times. Each year brings more and more. Topping it off, imagine the confusion when an English-learner turns to the dictionary for help, looks up the very word "jargon," and finds it defined as "a smoky, yellow, or colorless variety of zircon."

You couldn't blame him for considering all of us *Depps*.

Slang: Leapin' Lizards or _____ You?

Whether you are a folksy cusser or a four-letter one, the time for slang of any kind is *never* during business hours. Even if the scene is dinner or drinks and the company the oldest of friends, chances of misinterpretation are too great. A "gee whillikers" kind of remark, even in London, often simply draws a blank, while a saltier phrase, however amicably intended, may easily be misread as a serious insult.

In Islamic and Buddhist cultures, a mere "thank God" is taken as blasphemy unless unmistakably meant piously, while any interjection with sexual overtones will surely bring the wrath of Allah down on you. But religious strictures aside, there is always the risk of coming off as too casual, nervy, or disrespectful.

The You Nobody Knows

What happens when the last briefcase is snapped shut and your hosts invite you out on the town? Do you remain Mary Poppins or do you let King Kong out of the cage?

Often, when business seems to be officially over, it is actually just beginning. Your overseas hosts expect you to relax and reveal a little more of the real you. In fact, that may be the whole point. The rollicking businessman's binge is a standard tactic, especially in Japan, for sizing up the other side. Whether at the conference table, on the golf course, or in a geisha house, avoid any expletives you may regret the next morning. Remember that even if he was not at the party, the top man you are dealing with is very much aware that *you* were.

One U.S. traveler recalls good-naturedly dropping a few X-rated monosyllables while out with a Malaysian customer, who a few days later turned inexplicably surly. The problem? Without understanding its precise implications, the Malay had taken a fancy to one of the American's zingers and later had sprung it on one of his own customers, who did indeed understand. Bad news for both East *and* West.

It isn't just expletives that can get you into trouble, either. We forget that many of our slangiest expressions have had the four-letter words bleeped out of them (as in "mother" and "hit the fan"). But if your audience has not forgotten, the effect will be much harsher than you intended. The same goes for words that, over here, may seem perfectly bland (as in "smart ass") but in different surroundings can be quite shocking. Even "belly up," according to several Americans back from overseas, invariably draws snickers or blank stares.

Avoid the usual ephemera such as "with it," "go for it," and "no way," not only because they are unimaginative to begin with but also because they are old hat before the rest of the world has ever heard them. Even slang that has survived for generations may still have never left the country.

Another innocent abroad gave his order in a Japanese restaurant, then changed his mind and called the waiter back. "Scratch the sushi," he said. The sushi was, of course, promptly served — presumably properly scratched, as ordered.

Officialese: Shorter Is Not Always Clearer

"Found under carnal knowledge," the legendary charge brought against Elizabethan adulterers (though actually coined at the start of *this* century), inspired the world's first acronym to really catch on. Still the most popular of them all, it is now daddy to a huge litter of late-twentieth-century progeny.

From MASH, MERV, and MOMA to CAD/CAM, FYI, ASAP, and SWAK, civilization takes great pride in squeezing a few self-explanatory words into a squat chunk of capital letters, which take on a life of their own so fast that the words they stand for shrivel and fall away like husks from autumn corn. Maybe it is all part of progress and conservation — shorter words, fewer pages, less deforestation.

But unless everybody knows what you are shortening, the best policy is length — even if you have to spell out ILGWU or ASCAP. If nothing else, it serves to remind *us* what we are talking about.

The same goes for abbreviations such as R and R, and P and L, and CEO, which are basic English to us, alphabet soup to everyone else. Only when you are referring to the same thing over and over is it safe to revert to initials.

Humor: One Man's Mede is Another Man's Persian

Just don't try out S. J. Perelman's famous pun on an Iranian, for one culture's dazzling wordplay is another's dud. If Gorgonzola can cross vast oceans, why can't a joke make it safely across Forty-second Street without curdling?

Because humor is an acquired — and very perishable — taste. While to a Frenchman the essence of humor is an aphorism from La Rochefoucauld, nine out of ten Americans think La Rochefoucauld is goat cheese. Not that anyone arrives in Hong Kong cracking "flied lice" jokes or in Poznan asking, "How many Poles does it take . . . " But truly tasteless jokes are not the only yuks to leave at home.

Humor need not stalk the streets in a ski mask to alienate aliens. Mots dressed up in banker's gray and academic tweeds are just as unwelcome at border crossings. Puns, double entendres, irony, sarcasm, Oscar Wilde, Dorothy Parker, and Johnny Carson remain unexportable.

Looks like it's going to rain "cats and dogs."

I Never Mediterranean I Didn't Like

Ha ha. Except in the Mediterranean. Ethnic slurs can be detected where you never meant them. Affecting an accent like your host's, for example, though intended as a friendly joke or even as a compliment, will almost certainly be taken as an insult. Never try to get a chuckle at the expense of the national cuisine or architecture or government. And although it is safe for the locals to ridicule their own traffic jams and smog and the plumpness of their women, these are not for us to notice, much less crack wise about.

Or, as an Atlantan who covers the world for his securities firm reminds us, "If there is one thing that isn't funny in a foreign country, it's humor." Yours, that is.

Vocabulary and Grammar: Right Idea/Wrong Word

Most English-speaking foreigners with whom we deal are at the mercy of a limited vocabulary and rudimentary sentence structure. Yet the English they can speak is frequently more technically correct than ours! After all, they were taking lessons long after we parsed our last sentence in sixth grade. They wouldn't dream of dangling a participle or misplacing a modifier, while we break so many rules that we have come to speak a broken English all our own. We understand it, but does anyone else?

The American who says "infer" when he means "imply" leaves his listeners stumped, not because of what they *don't* know but because they do know the words have exactly opposite meanings.

They also know that "hardly," "scarcely," and "barely" are negative themselves and therefore never belong with a "not." So when the American says, "I couldn't read hardly a word of your contract," his listeners breathe a sigh of relief. Unbeknownst to himself, he has just told them he had no trouble at all with the contract.

Word-wise, Sentence Foolish

Anybody with a few English lessons under his belt can tell you what "wise" means — except when you tack it onto another word, as in, "Diesel-wise, this machine outperforms everything else on the road." A wise diesel? Maybe your customer would rather have a dumb but reliable one.

Another factor contributing volumes to international misunderstanding is our native exuberance. Call something "fantastic" or "fabulous" and an unsuspecting foreigner may think you mean unreal or imaginary. To us a disaster can be anything slightly less than perfect ("Lunch was a disaster — they ran out of fresh chives"). People on other continents think of disaster as pestilence, war, famine, and death.

We also tend to overdramatize both friend and foe with descriptions like "idiot," "clown," "slave driver," and "prince." Again, we forget that our audience only knows what they read in their pocket dictionary.

Don't Ask for the Little Girl's Room in Minsk

The other side of the too-graphic coin is not-nearly-graphic-enough. Why is a nation of pioneers and log splitters terrified of the word toilet? "Bathroom," "rest room," "powder room," "comfort station" — all are likely to be taken literally by foreigners, who will tell you, "Sorry, but we don't have one of those." Say that you want to "wash up" and you may be given a hot towel. Calling a toilet a toilet is particularly useful when making hotel reservations, because even in Paris many hotel rooms, though almost always equipped with a sink (and even a bidet), do not have a toilet closer than the end of the hall.

All the words we use should be simple and straightforward, not just the touchy ones. And, above all, make sure *you* understand them before springing them on alien ears. In a schedule of events at a petroleum convention in Houston, it was announced, "Alumni from all United States universities can conjugate and sit together . . . ." Foreign delegates who checked the meaning of conjugate in the dictionary no doubt spent the afternoon in the bar.

Sentences should be not only short and simple but almost audibly punctuated. You can't say a comma or a semicolon unless you are Victor Borge, but you can use pauses and full stops to break up each thought into chewable bits the same way dots and dashes do.

Me Tarzan, You Jane

Simplicity can, of course, be overdone. Never go on to the next point until the last one is thoroughly understood. But never speak condescendingly, either. When pausing to ask if your listeners got it, either do it lightly ("It's a complicated subject. Did I go too fast?") or put the onus on yourself ("Sometimes I speak too quickly. Shall I go over that again?")

No matter how wide a communications gap you face, you will never bridge it sounding like a teacher of enunciation.

Other Languages, Other Misunderstandings

Our own language may be a pesky traveling companion, but when we get where we're going we are in for even more problems. Foreign usages have a way of sabotaging the best-laid English sentence — even in England.

For instance, the general manager of his firm's international division tells of complimenting a distinguished English gentleman on the knickers he was wearing. Why did the gentleman turn crimson? In Britain knee-length trousers are called "plus fours," while "knickers" are ladies' underpants.

Misunderstandings flow the other way, too. When an Englishman says that the project will be finished "at the end of the day," he simply means that it will be done when it's done — which could take six months. Even a word as unambiguous as "backlog" can convey the wrong impression. To the British a large backlog implies not a wonderful list of orders waiting to be filled but a hopelessly overstocked inventory someone was too inefficient to move off the shelves. Much to the surprise of a Magnavox representative at a London meeting, when he suggested "tabling" the next item on the agenda his host immediately began to discuss it; the verb turns out to have the opposite meaning over there. Tell a Londoner you want to "fill him in," and he thinks you are going to hit him over the head. Say, "My presentation bombed" in America and you mean, of course, that it failed. In London the term "bomb" means just the opposite — a great success.

Innocent little words can trip you up in Spanish-speaking countries as well. "Discuss," for example, sounds like the Spanish word *discutir*, which presupposes disagreement and hence connotes that you want to argue rather than just plain discuss. "Support" often strikes the Spanish sensibility as hinting at financial aid — not a wise commodity to ask a client or a government official to lend you. In case you do say the wrong thing, do not try to say you are embarrassed in what seems like proper Spanish — *Estoy embarazado*. It means you are pregnant.

On the other hand, when a Frenchman "demands" something, no offense should be taken. The French verb for ask is *demander*. And when he says "actual," he probably means what the word means in French: "at present."

The word that gets Americans in Japan into the most trouble is "you." To a Japanese it is almost a violation of his territory — like jabbing a finger under his nose. At the very highest levels, Japanese businessmen do not expect to be addressed directly or even *looked* at directly. Those whom you deal with at other levels do not think in terms of self but of company. "What do *you* think?" is not the point. What the *company* thinks is.

Another Oriental phobia is "no." There is no real "no" in the Japanese language. Instead, there is a kind of unpleasant hiss or sad-faced "It is very difficult." If you ask, "Do you want any spares?" do not settle for less than, "No, I do not want any spares." If you end a question by asking, "No?" the Japanese says, "Yes," meaning, "Yes, I meant no." In other words, he is saying that yes, he understands; not yes, he'll comply.

Lastly, even unsuspecting words can spring traps. An American told his Japanese customer, "Our thinking is in parallel." The Japanese agreed, but after many months nothing happened. Frustrated, the American asked, "Why didn't you act? We agreed our thinking was in parallel." The Japanese responded, "Yes, but I looked up the word parallel in the dictionary and it said 'two lines that never touch.'"

Interpreting Interpreters

Why struggle to make yourself understood when you can hire a multilingual whiz to do it for you?

As discussed in an earlier section, handing your thoughts over to someone else to express can be as risky as letting a backseat driver reach over your shoulder and do the steering. Does he know exactly where you want to go? And is he seeing the road from the same perspective you are? Unless you have been doing your act together for a long time, it is hard to tell.

A more or less correct translation of your *words* can badly betray your *sentiments*. "Can you give me your answer today?" isn't very different from "Give me your answer today"— yet one sounds reasonable, the other pushy and demanding. Expressing a question by the intonation of your voice ("These are your lowest estimates?") does not guarantee that it will come out a question in the other language.

If you are using technical language of any kind, even just normal business terms such as "Xerox," "stat," "round figure," or "blue pencil," do not depend on a professional interpreter to know the proper translation. Also, do not expect him/her to admit to not knowing. Like everybody else, they are paid for what they know, not for what they have to look up in the dictionary.

Nor is it possible for most Americans to tell how an interpreter sounds to the other side. For instance, if he is from Spain, his standard Castilian Spanish will probably strike an Argentine or Mexican as "too Spanish" and hence daunting— like a cockney being lectured by someone with an Oxbridge accent. And the accent of a Latin American can grate on a Castilian's ear like a snapped guitar string. The French, too, are supersensitive to regional French accents. A Parisian may have an adverse reaction to a Toulouse translator without even being conscious of it.

So Whom Can You Trust?

Beware of interpreters provided by the other side. Not that they are deliberate saboteurs, but it is only human to harbor a bias in favor of one's own employer. They may instinctively overlook nuances that express urgency, irritation, or even diffidence. Particularly in the Far East, where the urge to please submerges most other motivations, your go-between is likely to be reluctant to carry a message for you.

And, should you be lucky enough to discover the mistranslation before it is too late, how can you complain when the translator is your client's right-hand man?

One director of his company's international trade division hit on a solution. First, he created a new title: corporate interpreter. Then he gave the job to a young Japanese studying for his Ph.D. over here. Not only was the Oriental's English nearly flawless, but he was ambitious enough to master both the technical side of the company *and* its corporate culture. "He is no mere set of vocal chords," says the director proudly; "he's a business consultant."

Traveling Checklist

1. **The eyes have it.** Keep a constant lookout for the glazed expression and the wandering or sleepy eye that tell you that you have lost your audience.

2. **"Is that perfectly clear?"** Don't guess, ask. Nods and smiles do not necessarily signify understanding.

3. **Stop and start.** Don't wait until the end of a speech or even a sentence before checking for comprehension. Never go on to *B* until *A* is thoroughly grasped.

4. **Spot quiz.** Don't take yes for an answer. Ask probing questions that prove how much your listener is really absorbing.

5. **After office hours.** If possible, meet with your opposite number for a quiet one-on-one double check of understanding on both sides.

6. **Shortcut shortcuts.** Avoid "i.e.," "ditto," "etc.," etc. Say "we will" instead of "we'll" and "I believe your proposal is not acceptable" instead of "I don't believe your proposal is acceptable."

Plus These Quickies

- Enunciate distinctly and slowly.
- Overpunctuate with pauses and full stops.
- Make one point at a time, one sentence at a time.
- Paraphrase and ask others to do the same.
- Avoid questions that can be answered yes or no.
- If there is a misunderstanding, take the blame.
- Use visual aids (photos, sketches, diagrams, graphs).
- Use both languages in visual presentations like flip charts, videotapes, and slide shows.
- Put what you are going to say in writing *before* you say it.
- Write and distribute a report on what was said as soon as possible after the meeting.
- Never use numbers without writing them out for all to see.
- If possible, say numbers in both languages.
- Send a follow-up telex, fax or letter to confirm what was said by telephone.
- Let your host set the pace of negotiations.
- Greet foreigners in their language, especially if it is an uncommon one like Arabic, Urdu, or Hindi.
- In Japan learn terms of greeting and departure phonetically so you will be understood.
- Take a foreign-language cassette with you to practice pronunciation as you go along.
- Do not speak whole sentences in a language you have not thoroughly mastered.
- One exception to the above: "Where is the toilet?"

- Never interrupt.
- Don't ask rhetorical questions — give your listener a chance to reply.
- Adjust the level of your English to your counterpart's.
- Finally, whatever you may think, booze does *not* make communication smoother or easier.

A Quickie Quiz

Have we raised your level of lingo consciousness?

Within the text you have just finished on lingo were these examples of Americanese that will cause confusion, not clarity, among non-Americans. Did you catch them?

> *Dr. Seuss*
> *Bazooka gum*
> *Madison Avenue*
> *cornflakes*
> *Hula Hoop*
> *Willy Loman*
> *Herschel Walker*
> *EEG*
> *the red-eye (flight)*
> *Rodeo Drive*
> *blew out to Catalina*
> *Houstonized*
> *Mary Poppins*
> *King Kong*
> *X-rated*
> *Forty-second Street*
> *Victor Borge (and his famous phonetic punctuation)*
> *backseat driver*

If you spotted these, if you became aware that American colloquialisms were being used in a chapter devoted to becoming more sensitized to them, then score yourself an *A*.

Homework

1. Learn another language.
2. Learn to speak your own language better by *writing* it better.
3. Learn more about the new world to which you are going.

A list of sources for help in all aspects — language, writing, and cross-cultural instruction — can be found in the Appendix.

TURNING THE TIDE

Tips for
*In*coming Visitors
to the U.S.

International business traffic flows both ways. So what happens when people from other shores arrive on ours? It can be just as confusing — to both sides — as any cultural breakdown experienced by American innocents abroad. To be sure, many foreigners high up enough in the corporate hierarchy to be sent here have almost certainly met their fair share of Americans as well as their own fellow nationals who have lived and worked here.

Yet a nation's entire ethos and idiosyncrasies cannot be absorbed long-distance. Hence, following are some trouble spots for foreigners to anticipate en route.

U.S. Protocol — Business and Personal

What is basically polite and considerate on the other side of the world translates the same way here, with minor variations and perhaps somewhat less emphasis on the formal and decorous.

Timing

U.S. business usually begins on the dot. A 9 A.M. appointment means precisely that, except in the most traffic-jammed big cities like New York, Houston, and Los Angeles, where a fifteen-minute delay is rarely frowned upon.

For social engagements, even with business motivations, "drinks at seven" implies something more like seven-thirty. But "dinner at eight" means eight, traffic or no traffic. Business meetings over lunch are the rule rather than the exception and usually start by twelve-thirty and end by two. In America lunch is rarely a heavy meal of many courses, for the regular workday continues immediately afterward. Dinner is the main meal, starting between seven and nine unless a cocktail party has preceded it, in which case it might not get going until ten — but rarely later.

Don't be surprised to get breakfast invitations. It is becoming the most popular time of day for intimate business get-togethers and signifies no slight. "Brunch," which is popular on weekends, is a combination meal that starts as early as eleven and can still be had at four. The fare ranges from scrambled eggs to sirloin steak, and the drinks tend to be the fruity-vegi type, such as screwdrivers (vodka and orange juice), mimosas (champagne and orange juice), and Bloody Marys (vodka mixed with highly spiced tomato juice). Note: If you wish to be sociable but not imbibe alcohol, one common substitute is a Virgin Mary, or the spiced tomato juice without any alcohol.

No matter what time of day, though, as soon as everyone is seated expect only the briefest exchange of small talk before the Americans get right down to business. No sipping tea or feeling one another out in the U.S.

Hands across the sea

American men invariably shake hands during introductions — women, not as often. *Abrazos*, bowing, and hand kissing are trotted out only by those who have spent years in another culture where such gestures are common. A peck on the cheek is only exchanged between women or between men and women — and then only after considerable acquaintance.

More and more women are entering the American business world and are making it to some of the highest levels. Women expect the man to let them take the initiative in shaking hands. If the occasion is business, they will almost certainly offer a hand. If it is social, you never know, but it is very rude not to be ready with a hand when invited.

When the chairman isn't

Most businesswomen realize that they are still a novelty to the foreign men they deal with. However, they do not welcome being treated like creatures from another galaxy — or like decoration. The best policy is to ignore gender altogether and proceed as you would with any male colleague. Helping with doors and chairs is fine as long as it does not become too attention-getting. If the woman reaches for the check, react exactly as you would with anyone else; if you are the client, chances are you expect to be treated — so let her do the treating.

With or without others present, never get as personal as you might with a male colleague. And that includes asking about her marital status — leave it to her to establish it, and if she does, a few casual questions about children or husband's occupation are as far as you should go with it.

Needless to say, amorous or suggestive remarks will get you a very cold shoulder 99.9 percent of the time; and can the other .1 percent be worth it?

"Who you?"

In some languages, including English English, "What do you do?" translates as insulting at best. But in America it is the standard opening line when people meet socially. It means, of course, "What kind of work do you do, and for whom do you do it?" Be prepared for it — it won't go away.

Most businesspeople carry business cards, but in the U.S. they are exchanged not automatically on meeting but usually only if there is some reason to want to get in touch later. No one will refuse *your* card, but do not be offended if you are not given one in return.

When being entertained at an American home, the most common gesture of gratitude is to send a short, informal note to the hostess after the event. Bringing a gift with you is risky, only because it might embarrass other guests who did not. But if you do bring something, potted or cut flowers or a bottle of wine are the safest, although a bouquet of flowers gives the hostess, who will very likely have no hired help, yet another chore just as she is coping with drinks, dinner, and introductions.

Probably the most charming commodity you can come equipped with is a toast or saying from your own culture, to be delivered bilingually as a salute to your host and hostess. It is something they cannot buy at the local supermarket, and invariably they and the other guests lap it up like pink champagne.

To puff or not to puff

In the U.S., land of the five-cent cigar, smoking is becoming as controversial as publicly admitting that you love the president or hate him.

To be on the safe side, either ask if anybody minds or wait to see what the others do. Even some cabdrivers now post signs in the backseat demanding that passengers refrain. A friendly host will seldom do the same, although more businesses are adopting policies that forbid smoking indoors. Also, many restaurants now segregate smokers from nonsmokers, which can lead to an awkward decision. If you do and your American host does *not*, do you volunteer to go without a puff all through dinner — or does he sit in a miasma of smoke to accommodate your habit?

No third party can supply the answer (they haven't invented "smoking counselors" yet). You simply have to be sensitive to the other side's position and let your conscience (plus an eye to making a sale) be your guide.

Gestures Here and There

Generally, what signifies "Here's mud in your eye!" where *you* come from has the same impact where *we* come from. Two exceptions you will no doubt encounter are America's "okay" signs. One is thumbs up, and the other is thumb and forefinger joined to form a circle. Either way, don't start punching — the intent is positive. The same is true for the *V*-for-victory sign, which, fingers facing in or out, never means what it does in Britain.

Patting someone on the rear end is strictly taboo — even though you may see hulking football players do it regularly on TV every Sunday afternoon. (Even then, they mustn't linger.)

But all the other international rudenesses from third finger to forearm jerk have made the trip to the New World intact.

To motion a waiter for the check, make a writing gesture.

To signal to someone he has a telephone call, hold an imaginary phone to your ear.

To wish someone good luck, cross the middle finger over the forefinger.

To wave good-bye, instead of waggling the fingers, move the whole hand from side to side.

One uniquely American gesture as indigenous to some parts of the country as the black fly is the backslap. If it is any consolation to the rest of the world, many Americans dislike it just as much as you do. The best response is a slight but unmistakable wince.

Giving and Entertaining

Giving can be a worse mistake than not giving at all. Americans are still slightly jumpy from the payola scandals of the seventies, and any hint that a business decision might have been influenced by gifts casts a shadow over everyone involved. (After all, the head of the nation's National Security Council lost his job for accepting two Japanese watches.) Even the law discourages excess generosity, placing a twenty-five-dollar limit on the tax deductibility of business gifts.

There are two occasions (other than being entertained in someone's home, which calls for either a thank-you note or a small offering to the hostess such as flowers or wine) when a modest gift is a welcome sign of your cordiality.

One is Christmas Day, December 25, a holiday of traditional gift giving among family, friends, and business associates. If the gift is strictly business, it is best to limit it to something for the office: leather-bound desk diaries, calendars, pen and pencil sets, paperweights, etc. Unless you know the recipient is a teetotaler, liquor or wine is also appropriate. It is customary for the store to Christmas-wrap purchases any time after December 1, so you needn't worry about the right colors (red and green) or designs.

The other reason to give a gift is simply to mark your arrival or departure with a token. Usually, the most appreciated are those from home. *Your* home. Appropriate are something made of jade or other semiprecious native stone; a doily made of handwoven fabric; a national beverage such as aquavit from Scandinavia, pisco sour from Peru, or Armagnac from France; any inexpensive handicraft or artwork; or an illustrated book about your country, its people, or its art. Cheap trinkets from *any*where are an insult, especially when imprinted with your company's logo. This is like foisting a piece of advertising promotion on your host.

If the businessperson you are dealing with over here is a woman, avoid personal gifts such as perfume, clothing (except perhaps a scarf or handkerchief), and makeup. If you know before leaving home that you will meet your host's family, it is always appropriate to take a small homegrown gift for spouse or children: a silver coin from Mexico, niello from Thailand, carved animal figures, or a cookbook of native dishes if you know the recipient can read your language.

Business gifts should be given after negotiations are over, preferably on a social occasion like a last lunch or farewell drink. If the present is a personal one, never offer it while others are on hand unless it is well known that you and the recipient are old and close friends.

Don't be insulted if an American does not reciprocate immediately. It may not happen until you have returned home — or come back on your next trip. There is no particular time limit here for returning favors.

Probably the most common gift given and received in the U.S. is entertainment, a word that covers everything from a quick drink to a weekend at a resort. It in no way signifies that you must return tit for tat. Not only is it tax-deductible but it will no doubt go on your host's expense account. The proper response is a sincere thank-you and an offer to return the favor when your host visits you.

Postscript

There is one universal action, one signal, one form of communication that is used and understood by every culture and in every country, no matter how remote.

It can help you with every relationship — business or personal — and become the single most useful form of communication.

It is . . . the smile.

We hope that this book has brought you one or two of those.

Among all the do's and don'ts in international travel, the smile is a gigantic "do." It will help you through the toughest of times and make your travel or transactions the stimulating fun and challenge they should be.

THE EDITOR

APPENDIX

Sources
of
Help

Learning Another Language

Learning a second language presupposes that most of your business travels will be in one area where one language predominates. And not even a total-immersion course will produce results overnight. In fact, there is no teacher nearly as effective as living with the language in its own land.

Of course, there are less drastic alternatives. In the Manhattan telephone book alone, 68 different language schools are listed, not including individual tutors. Berlitz has branches in over 200 locations in the U.S. and elsewhere and is now developing a whole new curriculum of programs in cross-cultural training and orientation. For those in a hurry, there is a nine-hour-a-day, five-day-a-week program that lasts from two to six weeks. You emerge frazzled but reasonably fluent.

Most community colleges and universities and even some high schools with adult-education classes offer courses — usually in Western European languages. But people with demanding full-time jobs often find private tutoring the most flexible way to learn.

A number of schools and organizations offer language instruction as well as a variety of cross-cultural training programs for business executives traveling abroad. See pages 185-187 for programs in your area.

Don't assume that because your company has never volunteered to underwrite employees' language lessons they would not be open to at least sharing the cost. For starters you might ask them to buy a do-it-yourself cassette kit, which you and others in the firm could use as a warm-up — and to prove that you are serious about learning.

Speak Your Language Better
By Writing It Better

The better we write, the better we talk. Writing good business English comes not from acquiring technical skills but from organizing our thinking.

Again, local schools from preparatory to college level offer courses, and only one or two semesters in an extension program should be enough for most businesspeople to be writing — and speaking — a new brand of English. It is, however, a subject that many college graduates have no trouble teaching themselves. All you need is patience and a good book. Here is a list of some of the best books on the subject recently published or reissued.

Books on Writing

The Art of Writing Clearly; W.G. Ryckman; Dow Jones-Irwin Personal Learning Aid Series; 1983. This book takes you from the fundamentals of word usage to the fine art of writing lucid business reports.

British English, A to Zed; Norman W. Schur; HarperCollins: 1991. A must for anyone headed for the U.K., the book catalogs the colorful pitfalls of finding yourself in the land of the Queen's English.

The Elements of Style; William Strunk, Jr., and E. B. White; Macmillan; 1979. This is the book that "wrote the book" on the elements of style. It would be hard to find any book on any subject that says so much so well in just 92 paperback-style pages.

The Transitive Vampire; Karen Elizabeth Gordon; Times Books; 1984, and *The Enlarged Transitive Vampire*; Karen Elizabeth Gordon; Random House; 1993. Both of these volumes are subtitled *A Handbook of Grammar for the Innocent, the Eager & the Doomed.* Whether you fall into any or all of those categories, these whimsically illustrated books prove that grammar and punctuation can be more bizarre than boring.

Writing that Works; Kenneth Roman and Joel Raphaelson; HarperCollins; 1992. Two top advertising writers with Ogilvy & Mather have written a book just the way the title says it should be.

Learn about
The New World You Are Visiting

Columbus may have been the best-known traveler who didn't know where he was going, but he wasn't the last. We think nothing of flying for twenty hours at supersonic speeds only to reach a land that is a total political, cultural, and geographical blank to us.

While increasing numbers of American firms are starting to take the mystery out of the Mysterious East (and West) with employee indoctrination courses, all too often they are reserved for those going to live there. There is also, however, hope for those who are just visiting.

Training: Workshops, Instruction, Lectures, and Other Information Sources

The BCIU Institute (Business Council for International Understanding) at the American University (Washington, D.C.) educates and trains both Americans and foreign nationals to operate in other cultures. With over 25,000 graduates from technicians to corporate CEOs in 143 countries, it is the oldest organization in the business. Eighty percent of the programs are conducted in Washington, twenty percent on-site or overseas. For each client company, programs can be custom-designed for corporate staffs; negotiating teams; adults, teenagers, and children; reentering families; or foreign families coming to the U.S. Programs can be arranged for individuals, executives and their families, and larger groups. All staff members have country- and culture-specific experience and have worked and lived in the country for which they are experts. Programs can run from one day to several weeks and include intercultural communication, area and country studies, and/or language training through 43 different community-specific language learning systems.

James Bostain (Alexandria, Virginia), a linguist and trainer for the U.S. Department of State Foreign Service Institute, has won Emmy awards for his television programs on what he calls "cross-cultural communication." He delivers these same lectures live to groups from coast to coast.

The Department of Development of the State of Ohio, International Trade Division (ITD), promotes trade between Ohio companies and foreign companies through its office in Columbus and overseas trade offices in Europe and Asia. Experienced commercial officers in Columbus work directly with Ohio companies to identify overseas outlets for exporting Ohio products and services. ITD's overseas trade offices stay abreast of foreign business trends and opportunities and can provide Ohio companies with guidance about the most effective avenues to promote their products.

Griggs Productions (San Francisco, California) has produced an award winning series of films and videotapes called *Going International,* to help the American traveler as well as incoming foreign nationals become more effective in international business. Parts I and II focus on cultural differences in business. Parts III and IV deal with cultural shock and with unexpected difficulties that employees and families experience upon returning to the U.S. Parts V and VI are geared toward foreigners coming to the U.S. to live. Part VII offers tips on safe international travel.

The Intercultural Press (Yarmouth, Maine) publishes an extensive list of titles about cross-cultural interaction and communication, including country-specific information. Certain members of the organization are also available for consultation on issues such as supervisory styles and patterns of communication in multicultural organizations. (See also page 187.)

The International Business Center of New England (Boston, Massachusetts) sponsors meetings and workshops focused on international trade issues. The organization's goal is to help companies do more international business more profitably.

The Massachusetts Port Authority (Massport) Trade Development Unit (Boston, Massachusetts) provides a wide range of programs for New England businesses interested in expanding their export activities. Staff in Boston, Europe, Latin America, and Asia offer personalized export counseling: research, market entry strategies, industry analysis, and business partnering. They also lead New England businesses to trade shows and trade missions around the world, providing logistical support and intensive marketing and research. The Boston office offers an ongoing series of educational programs and sponsors "Access, " a world trade databank.

Renwick and Associates Incorporated (Carefree, Arizona) prepares clients for international business in training sessions that last from two days to two weeks.

The School for International Training (Brattleboro, Vermont) is the accredited college of world learning, founded in 1932 as the Experiment in International Living. The school offers undergraduate and graduate degree programs in addition to short-term training for corporate executives; courses are tailor-made to each participant's goals.

Thunderbird, The American Graduate School of International Management (Glendale, Arizona), was founded in 1946 by a group of international-minded citizens led by a lieutenant general determined to solve the problem of innocents abroad who were not prepared for international assignments. In addition to stressing foreign-language training, the school gives customized, concentrated programs embracing the whole spectrum of foreign culture shock. Customized cultural and business programs can be arranged for a few days up to weeks or months. (See also page 188.)

Communication Services, Helpful Publications

The David M. Kennedy Center for International and Area Studies of Brigham Young University (Provo, Utah) supplies quick studies in the challenges of international travel. Booklets include *Taming Travel Stress, The International Family, Coming Home Again,* and *Travel and International Law.* Also useful are the four-page briefings called *Culturgrams,* which detail the customs, manners, likes, and dislikes of the peoples of over 100 countries.

The District Export Council in your area of the U.S. is a group of experimental international business executives, appointed by the U.S. secretary of commerce, who volunteer their services. Contact the nearest district office of the Department of Commerce.

The Intercultural Press publishes a long list of valuable guides, including *Survival Kit for Overseas Living; International Negotiation: A Cross-Cultural Perspective;* and *World Class Service.* They also put out two popular series. One is titled *Update* and covers the globe (how to prepare to leave home, what to do on arrival, local regulations and business practices, etc.). The other series is called *Interacts* and analyzes how Americans do things differently from people of other cultures and how relationships are thus affected. (See also page 186.)

The International Language Institute Transemantics, Inc. (Washington, D.C.) stresses the study of kinesics, or body language, as a key to effective understanding of others. The institute also offers multilanguage support from translating and interpreting to multilingual typesetting and editing, adaptation of promotional literature to foreign markets, film and tape narration, and convention services. Information is held in strictest confidence whenever requested.

The International Society for Intercultural Education, Training and Research (SIETAR International) (1505 22nd St., N.W., Washington, D.C. 20037) is an association of professionals in the field of intercultural education, training, and research. The membership is devoted to intercultural understanding through nonpolitical avenues for contact between people and among educators, trainers, and researchers; for professional development; and for the exchange and dissemination of information and knowledge.

OmniLingua, Inc. (Cedar Rapids, Iowa), translates, typesets, and prints manuals, audiovisuals, and materials-ads. All work is checked for technical accuracy, grammar, and local flavor.

The Stanford Institute for Intercultural Communication publishes an extensive directory of selected resources on other cultures, including training services and publishers.

The Thunderbird Management Center, a department of the *American Graduate School of International Management,* conducts customized executive training programs for businesspeople in language and/or business procedure. (See also page 186.)

The Travel Reference Center of the College of Business and Administration at the University of Colorado (Boulder, CO) claims to have the largest collection of travel, tourism, and recreation research studies available in any one place in the U.S. It also provides, for a fee, literature searches, information on specific research questions, research assistance, and copies of articles, papers, and other information.

The U.S. Travel and Tourism Administration (Washington, D.C.) is part of the U.S. Department of Commerce and is headed by an undersecretary for that department. The USTTA offers a wide range of publications dealing mainly with tourism in the United States. It offers extensive information on numbers of visitors and where they come from and why.

One final source of names and addresses you can turn to overseas is the *consulate* or *trade mission* here of the nation you are visiting there. The trail can be circuitous — but worth it. For example, if you call the commercial office of the New York Consulate of the People's Republic of China, you may be given the name and address of the China United Trading Corporation, Ltd., in New York, which in turn may give you the name and address of the people you really want to talk to — China Trade Consultation and Technical Service Corp., Andingmenway, Beijing, China.

Recommended Books

General

Culture Shock; Times Books International. This excellent series of books covers several Far Eastern countries, including Korea (1988), Thailand, Japan (1982), Malaysia, and Singapore (1979).

The Economist Business Traveller's Guides; Prentice Hall Press. Separate books have been published under this title for these areas: Britain, France, Germany, China, Japan, Southeast Asia, the United States, and the Arabian Peninsula.

The International Businesswoman: A Guide to Success in the Global Marketplace; Marlene L. Rossman; Praeger Publishers; 1986.

The Safe Travel Book: A Guide for the International Traveler; Peter Savage; Lexington Books; 1988.

On Asia

Chinese Etiquette & Ethics in Business; Boye De Mente; NTC Business Books; 1989.

Dealing with the Chinese: A Practical Guide to Business Etiquette in the People's Republic Today; Scott D. Seligman; Warner Books; 1989.

Looking at Each Other; Marion E. Current and Choi Dong-ho; Seoul International Tourist Publishing Company; 1983.

The Travelers' Guide to Asian Customs & Manners; Kevin Chambers; Meadowbrook; 1988.

When Business East Meets Business West: The Guide to Practice and Protocol in the Pacific Rim; Christopher Engholm; John Wiley & Sons; 1991.

On Japan

Getting Your Yen's Worth: How to Negotiate with Japan, Inc.; Robert T. Moran; Gulf Publishing Co.; 1985.

Hidden Differences: Doing Business with the Japanese; Edward T. Hall and Mildred Reed Hall; Doubleday; 1987.

How to Do Business with the Japanese: A Strategy for Success; Mark Zimmerman; Random House; 1985.

Japanese Culture and Behavior; Takie Sugiyama Lebra and William P. Lebra, eds.; University of Hawaii Press; 1986.

Japanese Etiquette & Ethics in Business; Boye De Mente; Passport Books; 1987.

Japanese Language and Culture for Business and Travel; Kyoko Hijrida and Muneo Yoshikawa; University of Hawaii Press; 1987.

With Respect to the Japanese: A Guide for Americans; John C. Condon; Intercultural Press; 1984.

On Other Areas

HarperCollins Business Guide to Moscow; Harper & Row; 1990.

Robert T. Moran's Cultural Guide to Doing Business in Europe; 2nd edition; Michael Johnson and Robert T. Moran; Butterworth-Heinemann; 1992.

The Travelers' Guide to European Customs & Manners; Nancy L. Braganti and Elizabeth Devine; Meadowbrook; 1984.

The Travelers' Guide to Latin American Customs & Manners; Elizabeth Devine and Nancy L. Braganti; St. Martin's Press; 1988.

Understanding Arabs: A Guide for Westerners; Margaret K. Nydell; Intercultural Press; 1987.

Index

PRO
395.52
Do   Do's and Taboos Around
the World.

DATE DUE

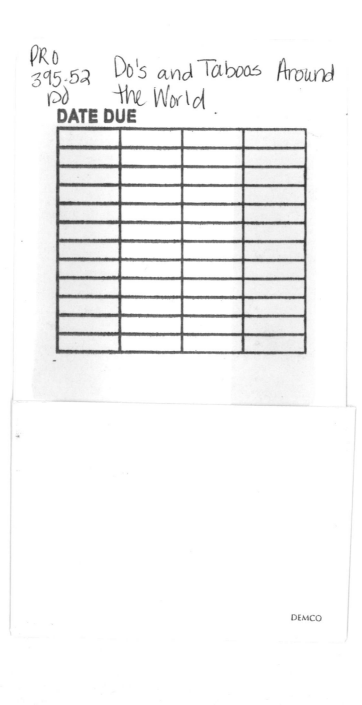